CONTENTS

INTRODUCTION

The Presto Electric Griddle

What is The Presto Electric Griddle?

An Presto electric griddle is a flat kitchen appliance that can be placed on a counter and used to prepare a variety of delicious meals. This device is made of cast iron and is partially coated with a non-stick coating. Electric griddles have an integrated heating element, while stovetop griddles are manufactured to heat by means of two-burner stoves. This appliance is easy to use, easy to clean and suitable for cooking a large quantity of food. With this cooking gadget, you can prepare pancakes, eggs, hamburgers, hot dogs and many quick dishes. A good feature of this kitchen appliance is its ability to prepare food without consuming too much electricity.Ceramic griddles are the right choice for a quick breakfast. With it you can prepare eggs, pancakes and bacon and at the same time toast bread in a toaster. The non-stick coating prevents food from sticking to the plate, so you don't have to add more fat to your meals.This device is easy to use, not difficult to operate, and even an inexperienced cook can find his way here. Most electric counter tops have heating settings that go from bottom to top so you can turn the dial and determine the temperature of the surface on which you want to cook. Also, the design of the electric griddle is quite practical. It has a lot of designs that are compatible with the kitchen decorations

How To Use Presto Electric Griddle Cookbook?

As already mentioned, the electric griddle is very easy to operate. I just want to give you some tips on how to find the easiest product to use.First of all, for new users of the electric griddle, you want to start with something simple. Pancakes are very simple, you can start with them. Put a little oil on the plate and preheat the plate to about 350 degrees. After confirming that it is hot, you can lower the temperature of the plate before pouring the dough. Turn the pancake when it starts to simmer until ready.In addition, the dish can be used to prepare different foods at the same time. After baking a batch of pancakes on the plate, you can clean the surface and prepare scrambled eggs. It is not necessary to use a griddle for dinner or full breakfast.Finally, if you use the griddle for thicker foods, it is best to use aluminum foil to package the food. When preparing foods such as ham, steaks, meat and pizza in a roasting dish, wrap it in foil and wrap it in slices of vegetables or potatoes.

The Best Electric Griddle: Presto Electric Tilt-n-Fold Griddle

What We Liked:

If you are in the market for a solid electric griddle to help step up your brunch game, then the Presto Tilt-n-Fold is a great choice. It has the largest cooking surface area of our top three models (253 square inches), solid cooking performance, and adjustable legs for easy grease runoff. It can also be easily cleaned and stored away, and it only costs around $50 (at the time of publication). That's a great deal for an appliance that most people will probably use once a week at most.

What We Didn't Like:

The Tilt-n-Fold griddle has a cold spot at the center of the cooking surface, which means one out of every nine pancakes will be paler than the others (or take the hint and only cook eight pancakes per batch). While that isn't ideal, it's also not a dealbreaker for us. The legs of the Tilt-n-Fold do fold up for storage, but it still takes up more room than the more affordable Presto 22-inch griddle (see below). The faux stainless steel border on the sides of the griddle became quickly stained with grease after a couple of rounds of cooking bacon and burgers. Even after intense scrubbing, we couldn't remove the stains, and didn't want to risk stripping away the coating.

Tips and Tricks on your Presto Electric Griddle

In general, most people an electric griddle to cook breakfast, such as bacon, eggs, steaks, and other types of meat. I'll suggest some other food tips that you can prepare with this device that are not quite expensive.

Crab cake

This cake is a good meal to prepare on the griddle, as it can be prepared in a single operation and not in batches. One of the biggest problems with batch baking is that at the end of the last batch, the first batch is either cold or a little dry from the oven.It is best to cook them all on the stove at the same time and prepare dinner in the blink of an eye without using the oven. Shrimp meal should be prepared on an electric griddle and ready to serve in less than 10 minutes.

Philadelphia Cheesesteak Sandwiches

It is an excellent meal that can be prepared in the blink of an eye. The impressive thing about preparing a cheesesteak in one dish is that you can do everything in one place and feel like a professional: the meat is cooked in one piece, the onions and the roast in another

Common FAQS about your Presto Electric Griddle

What temperature do you cook pancakes on an electric griddle?
With an electric griddle, 375 degrees is perfect. Tips: Test by making a one tablespoon pancake and adjust temperature accordingly. Not hot enough; slow cooking makes tough pancakes.

Can you wash an electric griddle?
Unplug your electric griddle and if the plate is removable, just wash it in soapy hot dish detergent. If your instruction manual states it's safe for the dishwasher, then put it there to clean. To wash by hand, do not use abrasives. A sponge or cloth will work fine.

Is griddle cooking healthy?
Ideal for summer lunches or a light meal if you prefer, cooking "a la plancha" is particularly healthy, quick and dietetics. Simply warm the dry plate before cooking. Foods are not fried but baked in their own juice, without adding fat.

BREAKFAST RECIPES

Mexican Eggs On Haystacks

Servings: 6

Cooking Time: 12 Minutes

Ingredients:

- ½ cup Breadcrumbs
- 3 ½ cups Store-Bought Hash Browns
- 2/3 cup Sour Cream
- 2 tsp Tex Mex Seasoning
- 6 Eggs
- 1/3 cup shredded Cheddar
- Salt and Pepper, to taste

Directions:

1. Preheat your grill to medium.
2. In the meantime, squeeze the hash browns to get rid of excess water, and place in a bowl.
3. Add the breadcrumbs, cheese, half of the Tex-Mex, and season with some salt and pepper.
4. Mix with your hands to combine.
5. Open the grill, unlock the hinge for the griddle, and lay it open. Spray with cooking spray.
6. Make six patties out of the hash brown mixture and arrange onto the griddle.
7. Cook for 7 minutes, flipping once, halfway through. Tarsnsfer to six serving plates.
8. Crack the eggs open onto the griddle, season with salt and pepper, and cook until they reach your preferred consistency.
9. Top the hash browns with the egg.
10. Combine the sourcream and remaining Tex Mex and top the eggs with it.
11. Enjoy!

Nutrition Info: Calories 340 ;Total Fats 21g ;Carbs 25g ;Protein 8.2g ;Fiber: 2g

Corn Cakes With Salsa And Cream Cheese

Servings: 8

Cooking Time: 8 Minutes

Ingredients:

- ½ cup Cornmeal
- ¼ cup Butter, melted
- ½ cup Salsa
- 14 ounces canned Corn, drained
- 1 cup Milk
- 6 ounces Cream Cheese
- 1 ½ cups Flour
- 6 Eggs
- ¼ cup chopped Spring Onions
- 1 tsp Baking Powder
- Salt and Pepper, to taste

Directions:

1. In a bowl, whisk together the eggs, butter, cream cheese, and milk.
2. Whisk in the cornmeal, flour, baking powder, salt, and pepper.
3. Fold in the remaining ingredients and stir well to incorporate.
4. Preheat your grill to medium.
5. When the light is on, unlock the hinge and lower to your counter.
6. Spray the griddle with a nonstick spray.
7. Ladle the batter onto the griddle (about ¼ of cup per cake).
8. When the cakes start bubbling, flip them over and cook until golden brown.
9. Serve as desired and enjoy!

Nutrition Info: Calories 325 ;Total Fats 15g ;Carbs 35g ;Protein 11g ;Fiber: 3g

Sausage And Mushroom Breakfast Skewers

Servings: 4

Cooking Time: 4 Minutes

Ingredients:

- 2 Italian Sausage Links
- 4 Whole White Button Mushrooms
- 1 Red Bell Pepper
- Salt and Pepper, to taste

Directions:

1. Soak four skewers in cold water for 2-3 minutes.
2. Preheat your grill to 375 degrees F.
3. Meanwhile, cut each sausage in eight pieces.
4. Quarter the mushrooms and cut the red pepper into eight pieces.
5. Sprinkle the mushrooms and pepper generously with salt and pepper.
6. Grab the skewers and thread the ingredients – sausage, mushroom, pepper, sausage mushroom, sausage mushroom, pepper, sausage, mushroom, in that order.
7. Place onto the grill and lower the lid.
8. Cook for 4 minutes closed.
9. Serve alongside some bread and a favorite spread and enjoy.

Nutrition Info: Calories 118 ;Total Fats 9.1g ;Carbs 4g ;Protein 7.3g ;Fiber: 0.6g

Classic Bacon And Eggs Breakfast

Servings: 1

Cooking Time: 8 Minutes

Ingredients:

- 2 Eggs
- 2 Bacon Slices
- 2 Bread Slices
- Salt and Pepper, to taste

Directions:

1. Preheat your grill to 400 degrees F, and make sure that the kickstand is in position.
2. When the light goes on, add the bacon to the plate and lower the lid.
3. Let cook for 4 full minutes.
4. Open the lid and crack the eggs onto the plate. Season with salt and pepper.
5. Add the bread slices to the plate, as well.
6. Cook for 4 minutes, turning the bread and bacon (and the eggs if you desire) over halfway through.
7. Transfer carefully to a plate. Enjoy!

Nutrition Info: Calories 434 ;Total Fats 19.6g ;Carbs 38.8g ;Protein 25.6g ;Fiber: 6g

Chocolate Chip And Blueberry Pancakes

Servings: 2

Cooking Time: 5 Minutes

Ingredients:

- 1 cup Pancake Mix
- ¼ cup Orange Juice
- 1/3 cup Fresh Blueberries
- ¼ cup Chocolate Chips
- ½ cup Water

Directions:

1. Preheat your grill to medium.
2. Meanwhile, combine the pancake mix with the orange juice and water.
3. Fold in the chocolate chips and blueberries.
4. Open the grill, unhinge, and lay the griddle onto your counter.
5. Spray with cooking spray.
6. Add about 1/6 of the batter at a time, to the griddle.
7. Cook until bubbles start forming on the surface, then flip over, and cook until the other side turns golden brown.
8. Serve and enjoy!

Nutrition Info: Calories 370 ;Total Fats 9g ;Carbs 66g ;Protein 3g ;Fiber: 3g

Grilled Ham Omelet

Servings: 2

Cooking Time: 5 Minutes

Ingredients:

- 6 Eggs
- 2 Ham Slices, chopped
- 2 tbsp chopped Herbs by choice
- ¼ tsp Onion Powder
- 1 tbsp minced Red Pepper
- ¼ tsp Garlic Powder
- Salt and Pepper, to taste

Directions:

1. Preheat your grill to 350 degrees F.
2. In the meantime, whisk the eggs in a bowl and add the rest of the ingredients to it. Stir well to combine.
3. Open the grill and unlock the hinge.
4. Coat the griddle with some cooking spray and gently pour the egg mixture onto it.
5. With a silicone spatula, mix the omelet as you would in a skillet.
6. When it reaches your desired consistency, divide among two serving plates.
7. Enjoy!

Nutrition Info: Calories 271 ;Total Fats 17.5g ;Carbs 2.4g ;Protein 24g ;Fiber: 0.1g

Quick Oat & Banana Pancakes

Servings: 4

Cooking Time: 5 Minutes

Ingredients:

- ½ cup Oats
- ¼ cup chopped Nuts by choice (Walnuts and Hazelnuts work best)
- 1 large Ripe Banana, chopped finely
- 2 cups Pancake Mix

Directions:

1. Preheat your grill to medium and unlock the hinge. Open it flat on your counter.
2. Meanwhile, prepare the pancake mix according to the instruction on the package.
3. Stir in the remaining ingredients well.
4. Spray the griddle with some cooking spray.
5. Drop about ¼ cup onto the griddle.
6. Cook for a minute or two, just until the pancake begins to puff up.
7. Flip over and cook for another minute or so – the recipe makes about 16 pancakes.
8. Serve as desired and enjoy!

Nutrition Info: Calories 310 ;Total Fats 8g ;Carbs 56g ;Protein 14g ;Fiber: 8g

VEGETARIAN RECIPES

Goat Cheese & Tomato Stuffed Zucchini

Servings: 8

Cooking Time: 8 Minutes

Ingredients:

- 14 ounces Goat Cheese
- 1 ½ cups Tomato Sauce
- 4 medium Zucchini

Directions:

1. Preheat your grill to medium-high.
2. Cut the zucchini in half and scoop the seeds out.
3. Coat the grill with cooking spray and add the zucchini to it.
4. Lower the lid and cook for 2 minutes.
5. Now, add half of the goat cheese first, top with tomato sauce, and place the remaining cheese on top. Place a piece of aluminum foil on top of the filling so you don't make a big mess.
6. Carefully lower the grill and cook for an additional minute.
7. Serve and enjoy!

Nutrition Info: Calories 170 ;Total Fats 11g ;Carbs 8.2g ;Protein 10.5g ;Fiber: 2.3g

Caprese Eggplant Boats

Servings: 4

Cooking Time: 10 Minutes

Ingredients:

- 2 Eggplants
- 1 cup Cherry Tomatoes, halved
- 1 cup Mozzarella Balls, chopped
- 2 tbsp Olive Oil
- 4 tbsp chopped Basil Leaves
- Salt and Pepper, to taste

Directions:

1. Preheat your grill to 375 degrees F.
2. Cut the eggplants in half (no need to peel them- just wash well), drizzle with olive oil and season with salt and pepper, generously.
3. When the green light is on, open the grill and arrange the eggplant halves onto the bottom plate.
4. Lower the lid and cook for about 4-5 minutes, until well-done.
5. Transfer to a serving plate and top with cherry tomatoes, mozzarella and basil.
6. Serve and enjoy!

Nutrition Info: Calories 187 ;Total Fats 11g ;Carbs 18.3g ;Protein 6.8g ;Fiber: 7.3g

Spinach And Cheese Portobellos

Servings: 3

Cooking Time: 6 Minutes

Ingredients:

- 3 Portobello Mushrooms
- 2 cups Spinach, chopped
- 1 cup shredded Cheddar Cheese
- 4 ounces Cream Cheese
- 1 tbsp Olive Oil
- 1 tsp minced Garlic
- Salt and Pepper, to taste

Directions:

1. Preheat your grill to 350 degrees F.
2. Clean the mushroom caps well, and pat dry with paper towels.
3. Remove the stems, so the fillign can fit.
4. Now, make the filling by mixing the cheeses, spinach, and garlic. Divide this mixture among the mushrooms.
5. Drizzle with olive oil.
6. When the green light is on, open the grill and add the mushrooms.
7. Arrange on top of the plate and cook with the lid off for about 5 minutes.
8. Now, lower the lid gently, but do not use pressure. Let cook for 15-20 seconds, just so the cheese melts faster.
9. Transfer to a serving plate and enjoy!

Nutrition Info: Calories 210 ;Total Fats 9g ;Carbs 5g ;Protein 10g ;Fiber: 1g

Paprika & Chipotle Lime Cauli-steaks

Servings: 4

Cooking Time: 6 Minutes

Ingredients:

- 2 Cauliflower Heads
- 4 tbsp Olive Oil
- 1 tsp minced Garlic
- 1 tbsp Chipotle Powder
- 1 ½ tbsp Paprika
- 1 tsp Honey
- 1 tsp Salt
- Juice of 1 large Lime
- 1 tsp Lime Zest

Directions:

1. Preheat your grill to medium-high.
2. Remove the outter leaves of the cauliflower and trim them well. Lay them flat onto your cutting board and then cut into steak-like pieces. (about 3 to 4 inches thick).
3. In a bowl, whisk together all of the remaining ingredients.
4. Brush the steaks with the mixture well, and then arrange them onto the bottom plate of the grill.
5. Lower the lid to cut the cooking time in half, and cook only for about 6 minutes, without turning over.
6. Transfer to a serving plate and enjoy!

Nutrition Info: Calories 202 ;Total Fats 14g ;Carbs 16g ;Protein 6g ;Fiber: 8g

Basil Pizza

Servings: 2

Cooking Time: 7 Minutes

Ingredients:

- 1 pizza dough
- ½ tablespoon olive oil
- 1 cup pizza sauce
- 1½ cups part-skim mozzarella cheese, shredded
- 1½ cups part-skim provolone cheese, shredded
- 10 fresh basil leaves

Directions:

1. Place the water tray in the bottom of Presto Electric Griddle.
2. Place about 2 cups of lukewarm water into the water tray.
3. Place the drip pan over water tray and then arrange the heating element.
4. Now, place the grilling pan over heating element.
5. Plugin the Presto Electric Griddle and press the 'Power' button to turn it on.
6. Then press 'Fan" button.
7. Set the temperature settings according to manufacturer's directions.
8. Cover the grill with lid and let it preheat.
9. With your hands, stretch the dough into the size that will fit into the grilling pan.
10. After preheating, remove the lid and grease the grilling pan.
11. Place the dough over the grilling pan.
12. Cover with the lid and cook for about 2-3 minutes
13. Remove the lid and with a heat-safe spatula, flip the dough.
14. Cover with the lid and cook for about 2 minutes.
15. Remove the lid and flip the crust.
16. Immediately, spread the pizza sauce over the crust and sprinkle with both kinds of cheese.
17. Cover with the lid and cook for about 1 minute.
18. Remove the lid and cook for about 1 minute or until the cheese is melted.
19. Remove from the grill and immediately top the pizza with basil leaves.
20. Cut into desired sized wedges and serve.

Nutrition Info: (Per Serving):Calories 707 ;Total Fat 47.5 g ;Saturated Fat 23.1 g ;Cholesterol 80 mg ;Sodium 1000 mg ;Total Carbs 34.9 g ;Fiber 3.5 g ;Sugar 4.6 g ;Protein 35.8 g

Mediterranean Veggies

Servings: 4

Cooking Time: 10 Minutes

Ingredients:

- 1 cup mixed bell peppers, chopped
- 1 cup eggplant, chopped
- 1 cup zucchini, chopped
- 1 cup mushrooms, chopped
- ½ cup onion, chopped
- ½ cup sun-dried tomato vinaigrette dressing

Directions:

1. In a large bowl, add all ingredients and toss to coat well.
2. Refrigerate to marinate for about 1 hour.
3. Place the water tray in the bottom of Presto Electric Griddle.
4. Place about 2 cups of lukewarm water into the water tray.
5. Place the drip pan over water tray and then arrange the heating element.
6. Now, place the grilling pan over heating element.
7. Plugin the Presto Electric Griddle and press the 'Power' button to turn it on.
8. Then press 'Fan" button.
9. Set the temperature settings according to manufacturer's directions.
10. Cover the grill with lid and let it preheat.
11. After preheating, remove the lid and grease the grilling pan.
12. Place the vegetables over the grilling pan.
13. Cover with the lid and cook for about 8-10 minutes, flipping occasionally.
14. Serve hot.

Nutrition Info: (Per Serving):Calories 159 ;Total Fat 11.2 g ;Saturated Fat 2 g ;Cholesterol 0 mg ;Sodium 336 mg ;Total Carbs 12.3 g ;Fiber 1.9 g ;Sugar 9.5 g ;Protein 1.6 g

Vinegar Veggies

Servings: 4

Cooking Time: 10 Minutes

Ingredients:

- 3 golden beets, trimmed, peeled and sliced thinly
- 3 carrots, peeled and sliced lengthwise
- 1 cup zucchini, sliced
- 1 onion, sliced
- ½ cup yam, sliced thinly
- 2 tablespoon fresh rosemary
- 1 garlic clove, minced
- Salt and ground black pepper, as required
- 3 tablespoons vegetable oil
- 2 teaspoons balsamic vinegar

Directions:

1. Place all ingredients in a bowl and toss to coat well.
2. Refrigerate to marinate for at least 30 minutes.
3. Place the water tray in the bottom of Presto Electric Griddle.
4. Place about 2 cups of lukewarm water into the water tray.
5. Place the drip pan over water tray and then arrange the heating element.
6. Now, place the grilling pan over heating element.
7. Plugin the Presto Electric Griddle and press the 'Power' button to turn it on.
8. Then press 'Fan" button.
9. Set the temperature settings according to manufacturer's directions.
10. Cover the grill with lid and let it preheat.
11. After preheating, remove the lid and grease the grilling pan.
12. Place the vegetables over the grilling pan.
13. Cover with the lid and cook for about 5 minutes per side.
14. Serve hot.

Nutrition Info: (Per Serving):Calories 184 ;Total Fat 10.7 g ;Saturated Fat 2.2 g ;Cholesterol 0 mg ;Sodium 134 mg ;Total Carbs 21.5 g ;Fiber 4.9 g ;Sugar 10 g ;Protein 2.7 g

Grilled Pizza Margarita

Servings: 1

Cooking Time: 2 Minutes

Ingredients:

- 1 Tortilla
- 3 tbsp Tomato Sauce
- 3 ounces shredded Mozzarella
- 4 Basil Leaves, chopped
- Pinch of Salt

Directions:

1. Preheat your grill to medium-high.
2. Unlock to lower the griddle and lay it on your counter.
3. When the green light turns on, add the tortilla to the grill, and lower the lid.
4. Cook only for about 40 seconds, just until it becomes hot.
5. Add the tomato sauce on top, sprinkle with cheese, basil, and some salt.
6. Cook for another minute or so – with the lid OFF – until the cheese becomes melted.
7. Serve and enjoy!

Nutrition Info: Calories 375 ;Total Fats 22g ;Carbs 23g ;Protein 22g ;Fiber: 2g

Grilled Cauliflower

Servings: 4

Cooking Time: 40 Minutes

Ingredients:

- 1 large head of cauliflower, leaves removed and stem trimmed
- Salt, as required
- 4 tablespoons unsalted butter
- ¼ cup hot sauce
- 1 tablespoon ketchup
- 1 tablespoon soy sauce
- ½ cup mayonnaise
- 2 tablespoons white miso
- 1 tablespoon fresh lemon juice
- ½ teaspoon ground black pepper
- 2 scallions, thinly sliced

Directions:

1. Sprinkle the cauliflower with salt evenly.
2. Arrange the cauliflower head in a large microwave-safe bowl.
3. With a plastic wrap, cover the bowl.
4. With a knife, pierce the plastic a few times to vent.
5. Microwave on high for about 5 minutes.
6. Remove from the microwave and set aside to cool slightly.
7. In a small saucepan, add butter, hot sauce, ketchup and soy sauce over medium heat and cook for about 2-3 minutes, stirring occasionally.
8. Brush the cauliflower head with warm sauce evenly.
9. Place the water tray in the bottom of Presto Electric Griddle.
10. Place about 2 cups of lukewarm water into the water tray.
11. Place the drip pan over water tray and then arrange the heating element.
12. Now, place the grilling pan over heating element.
13. Plugin the Presto Electric Griddle and press the 'Power' button to turn it on.
14. Then press 'Fan" button.
15. Set the temperature settings according to manufacturer's directions.
16. Cover the grill with lid and let it preheat.
17. After preheating, remove the lid and grease the grilling pan.
18. Place the cauliflower head over the grilling pan.
19. Cover with the lid and cook for about 10 minutes.
20. Turn the cauliflower over and brush with warm sauce.
21. Cover with the lid and cook for about 25 minutes, flipping and brushing with warm sauce after every 10 minutes.
22. Transfer cauliflower to a plate and let cool slightly.
23. In a bowl, place the mayonnaise, miso, lemon juice, and pepper and beat until smooth.
24. Spread the mayonnaise mixture onto a plate and arrange the cauliflower on top.
25. Garnish with scallions and serve.

Nutrition Info: (Per Serving):Calories 261 ;Total Fat 22 g ;Saturated Fat 8.9 g ;Cholesterol 38 mg ;Sodium 1300mg ;Total Carbs 15.1 g ;Fiber 2.5 g ;Sugar 5.4 g ;Protein 3.3 g

Garlicky Mixed Veggies

Servings: 4

Cooking Time: 8 Minutes

Ingredients:

- 1 bunch fresh asparagus, trimmed
- 6 ounces fresh mushrooms, halved
- 6 Campari tomatoes, halved
- 1 red onion, cut into 1-inch chunks
- 3 garlic cloves, minced
- 2 tablespoons olive oil
- Salt and ground black pepper, as required

Directions:

1. In a large bowl, add all ingredients and toss to coat well.
2. Place the water tray in the bottom of Presto Electric Griddle.
3. Place about 2 cups of lukewarm water into the water tray.
4. Place the drip pan over water tray and then arrange the heating element.
5. Now, place the grilling pan over heating element.
6. Plugin the Presto Electric Griddle and press the 'Power' button to turn it on.
7. Then press 'Fan" button.
8. Set the temperature settings according to manufacturer's directions.
9. Cover the grill with lid and let it preheat.
10. After preheating, remove the lid and grease the grilling pan.
11. Place the vegetables over the grilling pan.
12. Cover with the lid and cook for about 8 minutes, flipping occasionally.

Nutrition Info: (Per Serving):Calories 137 ;Total Fat 7.7 g ;Saturated Fat 1.1 g ;Cholesterol 0 mg ;Sodium 54 mg ;Total Carbs 15.6 g ;Fiber 5.6 g ;Sugar 8.9 g ;Protein 5.8 g

Guacamole

Servings: 4
Cooking Time: 4 Minutes

Ingredients:

- 2 ripe avocados, halved and pitted
- 2 teaspoons vegetable oil
- 3 tablespoons fresh lime juice
- 1 garlic clove, crushed
- ¼ teaspoon ground chipotle chile
- Salt, as required
- ¼ cup red onion, chopped finely
- ¼ cup fresh cilantro, chopped finely

Directions:

1. Brush the cut sides of each avocado half with oil.
2. Place the water tray in the bottom of Presto Electric Griddle.
3. Place about 2 cups of lukewarm water into the water tray.
4. Place the drip pan over water tray and then arrange the heating element.
5. Now, place the grilling pan over heating element.
6. Plugin the Presto Electric Griddle and press the 'Power' button to turn it on.
7. Then press 'Fan" button.
8. Set the temperature settings according to manufacturer's directions.
9. Cover the grill with lid and let it preheat.
10. After preheating, remove the lid and grease the grilling pan.
11. Place the avocado halves over the grilling pan, cut side down.
12. Cook, uncovered for about 2-4 minutes.
13. Transfer the avocados onto cutting board and let them cool slightly.
14. Remove the peel and transfer the flesh into a bowl.
15. Add the lime juice, garlic, chipotle and salt and with a fork, mash until almost smooth.
16. Stir in onion and cilantro and refrigerate, covered for about 1 hour before serving.

Nutrition Info: (Per Serving):Calories 230 ;Total Fat 21.9 g ;Saturated Fat 4.6g ;Cholesterol 0 mg ;Sodium 46 mg ;Total Carbs 9.7 g ;Fiber 6.9 g ;Sugar 0.8 g ;Protein 2.1 g

Haloumi Kebobs

Servings: 4

Cooking Time: 5 Minutes

Ingredients:

- ½ pound Haloumi Cheese
- 4 Cremini Mushrooms, cut in half
- 1 Zucchini, cut into chunks
- ½ Bell Pepper, cut into chunks
- 2 tbsp Olive Oil
- Salt and Pepper, to taste

Directions:

1. Preheat your grill to 375 degrees F.
2. Meanwhile, soak 8 wooden skewers in water to preven burning.
3. Cut the cheese int chunks.
4. Thread the cheese and veggies onto the skewers, drizzle with the olive oil and sprinkle with salt and pepper.
5. Arrange onto the bottom plate, lower the lid, and cook closed for about 5 minutes (or more if you want it well-done).
6. Serve as desired and enjoy!

Nutrition Info: Calories 220 ;Total Fats 14g ;Carbs 6g ;Protein 5g ;Fiber: 1.2g

Buttered Corn

Servings: 6

Cooking Time: 20 Minutes

Ingredients:

- 6 fresh whole corn on the cob
- ½ cup butter, melted
- Salt, as required

Directions:

1. Husk the corn and remove all the silk.
2. Brush each corn with melted butter and sprinkle with salt.
3. Place the water tray in the bottom of Presto Electric Griddle.
4. Place about 2 cups of lukewarm water into the water tray.
5. Place the drip pan over water tray and then arrange the heating element.
6. Now, place the grilling pan over heating element.
7. Plugin the Presto Electric Griddle and press the 'Power' button to turn it on.
8. Then press 'Fan" button.
9. Set the temperature settings according to manufacturer's directions.
10. Cover the grill with lid and let it preheat.
11. After preheating, remove the lid and grease the grilling pan.
12. Place the corn over the grilling pan.
13. Cover with the lid and cook for about 20 minutes, rotating after every 5 minutes and brushing with butter once halfway through.
14. Serve warm.

Nutrition Info: (Per Serving):Calories 268 ;Total Fat 17.2 g ;Saturated Fat 10 g ;Cholesterol 41 mg ;Sodium 159 mg ;Total Carbs 29 g ;Fiber 4.2 g ;Sugar 5 g ;Protein 5.2 g

POULTRY RECIPES

Chicken Yakitori

Servings: 4
Cooking Time: 6 Minutes
Ingredients:

- 2 tbsp Honey
- 1 tsp minced Garlic
- 1-pound boneless Chicken
- 1 tsp minced Ginger
- 4 tbsp Soy Sauce
- Salt and Pepper, to taste

Directions:

1. In a bowl, combine the honey, ginger, soy sauce, and garlic. Add some salt and pepper.
2. Cut the chicken into thick stripes and add them to the bowl.
3. Mix until the meat is completely coated with the marinade.
4. Cover the bowl and refrigerate for about one hour.
5. Preheat your grill to medium.
6. Thread the chicken onto metal (or soaked wooden) skewers and arrange onto the bottom plate.
7. Lower the lid and cook for about 6-7 minutes, depending on how well-cooked you prefer the meat to be.
8. Serve and enjoy!

Nutrition Info: Calories 182 ;Total Fats 9g ;Carbs 10g ;Protein 27g ;Fiber: 0.2g

Seasoned Chicken Breast

Servings: 4

Cooking Time: 10 Minutes

Ingredients:

- 4 (4-ounce) boneless, skinless chicken breasts
- 1 teaspoon olive oil
- 1 teaspoon jerk seasoning

Directions:

1. Brush each chicken breast with olive oil and then rub with jerk seasoning.
2. Place the water tray in the bottom of Presto Electric Griddle.
3. Place about 2 cups of lukewarm water into the water tray.
4. Place the drip pan over water tray and then arrange the heating element.
5. Now, place the grilling pan over heating element.
6. Plugin the Presto Electric Griddle and press the 'Power' button to turn it on.
7. Then press 'Fan" button.
8. Set the temperature settings according to manufacturer's directions.
9. Cover the grill with lid and let it preheat.
10. After preheating, remove the lid and grease the grilling pan.
11. Place the chicken breasts over the grilling pan.
12. Cover with the lid and cook for about 3-5 minutes per side.
13. Serve hot.

Nutrition Info: (Per Serving):Calories 225 ;Total Fat 9.6 g ;Saturated Fat 2.5 g ;Cholesterol 101 mg ;Sodium 105 mg ;Total Carbs 0 g ;Fiber 0 g ;Sugar 0 g ;Protein 32.8 g

Grilled Chicken Breast

Servings: 2

Cooking Time: 12 Minutes

Ingredients:

- 3 tablespoons olive oil
- 5 fresh basil leaves, torn
- 1 clove garlic, sliced
- 2 chicken breasts, boneless, skinless
- Kosher salt and black pepper, to taste

Directions:

1. Rub the chicken breasts with black pepper, salt, garlic, basil leaves and olive oil.
2. Turn the "Selector" knob to the "Grill Panini" side.
3. Preheat the bottom grill of Presto Electric Griddle at 350 degrees F and the upper grill plate on medium heat.
4. Once it is preheated, open the lid and place the chicken breasts in the Griddler.
5. Close the griddler's lid and grill the skewers for 12 minutes.
6. Serve warm.

Nutrition Info: (Per Serving): Calories 453 ;Total Fat 2.4 g ;Saturated Fat 3 g ;Cholesterol 21 mg ;Sodium 216 mg ;Total Carbs 18 g ;Fiber 2.3 g ;Sugar 1.2 g ;Protein 23.2 g

Grilled Chicken Skewers

Servings: 4

Cooking Time: 5 Minutes

Ingredients:

- 1/4 cup fresh lime juice
- 2 garlic cloves, sliced
- 1 chipotle chile in adobo, chopped
- Kosher salt and black pepper, to taste
- 2 boneless chicken breasts, cut into chunks

Directions:

1. Mix chicken cubes with black pepper, salt, chile, garlic and lime juice in a bowl.
2. Thread the chicken cubes on the wooden skewers.
3. Turn the "Selector" knob to the "Grill Panini" side.
4. Preheat the bottom grill of Presto Electric Griddle at 350 degrees F and the upper grill plate on medium heat.
5. Once it is preheated, open the lid and place the skewers in the Griddler.
6. Close the griddler's lid and grill the skewers for 5 minutes.
7. Serve warm.

Nutrition Info: (Per Serving): Calories 440 ;Total Fat 7.9 g ;Saturated Fat 1.8 g ;Cholesterol 5 mg ;Sodium 581 mg ;Total Carbs 21.8 g ;Sugar 7.1 g ;Fiber 2.6 g ;Protein 37.2 g

Tequila Chicken

Servings: 3

Cooking Time: 7 Minutes

Ingredients:

- 1/2 cup gold tequila
- 1 cup lime juice
- 1/2 cup orange juice
- 1 tablespoon chili powder
- 1 tablespoon minced jalapeno pepper
- 1 tablespoon minced fresh garlic
- 2 teaspoons kosher salt
- 1 teaspoon black pepper
- 3 boneless chicken breasts

Directions:

1. Mix tequila, lime juice, orange juice, chili powder, jalapeno pepper, garlic, black pepper and salt in a bowl.
2. Add chicken breasts to the tequila marinade, cover and marinate for 1 hour.
3. Turn the "Selector" knob to the "Grill Panini" side.
4. Preheat the bottom grill of Presto Electric Griddle at 350 degrees F and the upper grill plate on medium heat.
5. Once it is preheated, open the lid and place the chicken breasts in the Griddler.
6. Close the griddler's lid and grill the chicken breasts for 7 minutes.
7. Serve warm.

Nutrition Info: (Per Serving): Calories 352 ;Total Fat 14 g ;Saturated Fat 2 g ;Cholesterol 65 mg ;Sodium 220 mg ;Total Carbs 15.8 g ;Fiber 0.2 g ;Sugar 1 g ;Protein 26 g

Marinated Chicken Breasts

Servings: 4

Cooking Time: 16 Minutes

Ingredients:

- ¼ cup extra-virgin olive oil
- 2 tablespoons fresh lemon juice
- 2 tablespoons maple syrup
- 1 garlic clove, minced
- Salt and ground black pepper, as required
- 4 (6-ounce) boneless, skinless chicken breasts

Directions:

1. For marinade: in a large bowl, add oil, lemon juice, maple syrup, garlic, salt and black pepper and beat until well combined.
2. In a large resealable plastic bag, place the chicken and marinade.
3. Seal the bag and shake to coat well.
4. Refrigerate overnight.
5. Place the water tray in the bottom of Presto Electric Griddle.
6. Place about 2 cups of lukewarm water into the water tray.
7. Place the drip pan over water tray and then arrange the heating element.
8. Now, place the grilling pan over heating element.
9. Plugin the Presto Electric Griddle and press the 'Power' button to turn it on.
10. Then press 'Fan" button.
11. Set the temperature settings according to manufacturer's directions.
12. Cover the grill with lid and let it preheat.
13. After preheating, remove the lid and grease the grilling pan.
14. Place the chicken breasts over the grilling pan.
15. Cover with the lid and cook for about 5-8 minutes per side.
16. Serve hot.

Nutrition Info: (Per Serving):Calories 460 ;Total Fat 25.3 g ;Saturated Fat 5.3 g ;Cholesterol 151 mg ;Sodium 188 mg ;Total Carbs 7.1 g ;Fiber 0.1 g ;Sugar 6.1 g ;Protein 49.3 g

Basil Grilled Chicken With Asparagus

Servings: 4

Cooking Time: 7 Minutes

Ingredients:

- 1 tsp Dijon Mustard
- 1 pound boneless and skinless Chicken Breasts
- 1 tsp dried Basil
- 1 tsp minced Garlic
- 2 tbsp Olive Oil
- ¼ tsp Onion Powder
- 12 Asparagus Spears
- Salt and Pepper, to taste

Directions:

1. Combine the oil, mustard, basil, garlic, onion powder, and some salt and pepper, in a bowl.
2. Coat the chicken with this mixture.
3. Meanwhile, preheat your grill to 350 degrees F.
4. Arrange the chicken breasts onto the bottom plate.
5. Season the asparagus with salt and pepper and add them next to the chicken.
6. Lower the lid, and cook closed, for 7 full minutes, or until your preferred doneness is reached.
7. Serve and enjoy!

Nutrition Info: Calories 350 ;Total Fats 24g ;Carbs 6g ;Protein 26g ;Fiber: 2g

Spiced Chicken Breasts

Servings: 4

Cooking Time: 14 Minutes

Ingredients:

- 2 scallions, chopped
- 1 (1-inch) piece fresh ginger, minced
- 2 garlic cloves, minced
- ¼ cup olive oil
- 2 tablespoons fresh lime juice
- 2 tablespoons low-sodium soy sauce
- 1 teaspoon ground cinnamon
- 1 teaspoon ground cumin
- 1 teaspoon ground turmeric
- Ground black pepper, as required
- 4 (5-ounce) boneless, skinless chicken breasts

Directions:

1. In a large Ziploc bag, add all the ingredients and seal it.
2. Shake the bag to coat the chicken with marinade well.
3. Refrigerate to marinate for about 20 minutes to 1 hour.
4. Place the water tray in the bottom of Presto Electric Griddle.
5. Place about 2 cups of lukewarm water into the water tray.
6. Place the drip pan over water tray and then arrange the heating element.
7. Now, place the grilling pan over heating element.
8. Plugin the Presto Electric Griddle and press the 'Power' button to turn it on.
9. Then press 'Fan" button.
10. Set the temperature settings according to manufacturer's directions.
11. Cover the grill with lid and let it preheat.
12. After preheating, remove the lid and grease the grilling pan.
13. Place the chicken breasts over the grilling pan.
14. Cover with the lid and cook for about 6-7 minutes per side
15. Serve hot.

Nutrition Info: (Per Serving):Calories 391 ;Total Fat 23.3 g ;Saturated Fat 4.7 g ;Cholesterol 126 mg ;Sodium 565 mg ;Total Carbs 2.7 g ;Fiber 0.7 g ;Sugar 0.7 g ;Protein 41.9 g

Chicken Burgers

Servings: 5
Cooking Time: 6 Minutes

Ingredients:

- 1 tablespoon butter, melted
- 1 small red onion, chopped
- 2 garlic cloves, chopped
- 2 tablespoons tomato paste
- 1 teaspoon sugar
- 1 tablespoon Worcestershire sauce
- 1 tablespoon hot sauce
- 1 1/4 pounds ground chicken
- 3 tablespoons olive oil
- 2 tablespoons honey

Directions:

1. Mix onion, butter, garlic, ground chicken, olive oil, honey, Worcestershire sauce, and sugar in a bowl.
2. Make the chicken patties out of this mixture.
3. Turn the "Selector" knob to the "Grill Panini" side.
4. Preheat the bottom grill of Presto Electric Griddle at 350 degrees F and the upper grill plate on medium heat.
5. Once it is preheated, open the lid and place the patties in the Griddler.
6. Close the griddler's lid and grill the patties for 6 minutes.
7. Serve warm.

Nutrition Info: (Per Serving): Calories 529 ;Total Fat 17 g ;Saturated Fat 3 g ;Cholesterol 65 mg ;Sodium 391 mg ;Total Carbs 55 g ;Fiber 6 g ;Sugar 8 g ;Protein 41g

Lemon And Rosemary Turkey And Zucchini Threads

Servings: 4

Cooking Time: 7 Minutes

Ingredients:

- 1-pound Turkey Breasts, boneless and skinless
- 1 Large Zuchinni
- 2 tbsp Lemon Juice
- ½ tsp Lemon Zest
- ¼ cup Olive Oil
- 1 tbsp Honey
- 1 tbsp Fresh Rosemary
- ¼ tsp Garlic Powder
- Salt and Pepper, to taste

Directions:

1. Cut the Turkey into smaller chunks, and place inside a bowl.
2. Add the olive oil, lemon juice, zest, honey, rosemary, garlic powder, and some salt and pepper, to the bowl.
3. With your hands, mix well until the turkey is completely coated with the mixture.
4. Cover and let sit in the fridge for about an hour.
5. Wash the zucchini thoroughly and cut into small chunks. Season with salt and pepper.
6. Preheat your Grill to 350 – 375 degrees F.
7. Thread the turkey and zucchini onto soaked (or metal) skewers and arrange on the bottom plate.
8. Lower the lid and cook closed for 6-7 minutes.
9. Serve and enjoy!

Nutrition Info: Calories 280 ;Total Fats 23g ;Carbs 6g ;Protein 27g ;Fiber: 0.5g

Meatballs Kabobs

Servings: 4

Cooking Time: 14 Minutes

Ingredients:

- 1 yellow onion, chopped roughly
- ½ cup lemongrass, chopped roughly
- 2 garlic cloves, chopped roughly
- 1½ pounds lean ground turkey
- 1 teaspoon sesame oil
- ½ tablespoons low-sodium soy sauce
- 1 tablespoon arrowroot starch
- 1/8 teaspoons powdered stevia
- Salt and ground black pepper, as required

Directions:

1. In a food processor, add the onion, lemongrass and garlic and pulse until chopped finely.
2. Transfer the onion mixture into a large bowl.
3. Add the remaining ingredients and mix until well combined.
4. Make 12 equal sized balls from meat mixture.
5. Thread the balls onto the presoaked wooden skewers.
6. Place the water tray in the bottom of Presto Electric Griddle.
7. Place about 2 cups of lukewarm water into the water tray.
8. Place the drip pan over water tray and then arrange the heating element.
9. Now, place the grilling pan over heating element.
10. Plugin the Presto Electric Griddle and press the 'Power' button to turn it on.
11. Then press 'Fan" button.
12. Set the temperature settings according to manufacturer's directions.
13. Cover the grill with lid and let it preheat.
14. After preheating, remove the lid and grease the grilling pan.
15. Place the skewers over the grilling pan.
16. Cover with the lid and cook for about 6-7 minutes per side.
17. Serve hot.

Nutrition Info: (Per Serving):Calories 276 ;Total Fat 13.4 g ;Saturated Fat 4 g ;Cholesterol 122 mg ;Sodium 280 mg ;Total Carbs 5.6 g ;Fiber 0.6 g ;Sugar 1.3 g ;Protein 34.2 g

Duck Veggie Kebobs

Servings: 2

Cooking Time: 7 Minutes

Ingredients:

- 8 ounces boneless and skinless Duck (breast is fine)
- 1/2 small Squash
- ½ Zucchini
- 1 small Red Bell Pepper
- ¼ Red Onion
- 2 tbsp Olive Oil
- 1 tbsp Balsamic Vinegar
- 2 tsp Dijon Mustard
- 2 tsp Honey
- Salt and Pepper, to taste

Directions:

1. Whisk together the oil, vinegar, mustard, honey, and some salt and pepper, in a bowl.
2. Cut the duck into chunks and dump into the bowl.
3. Mix to coat well and set aside. You can leave in the fridge for an hour or two, but if you are in a hurry, you can place on the grill straight away – it will taste great, as well.
4. Cut the veggies into chunks.
5. Plug the grill in, and set the temperature to 375 degrees F.
6. Thread the duck and veggies onto metallic skewers.
7. Open the grill and place on the bottom plate.
8. Lower the lid and cook for 5-8 minutes, depending on how done you want the meat to be.
9. Serve and enjoy!

Nutrition Info: Calories 250 ;Total Fats 10g ;Carbs 11g ;Protein 30g ;Fiber: 2g

Lemon Grilled Chicken Thighs

Servings: 4
Cooking Time: 6 Minutes

Ingredients:

- Juice and zest of 2 lemons
- 2 sprigs fresh rosemary, chopped
- 2 sprigs fresh sage, chopped
- 2 garlic cloves, smashed and chopped
- 1/4 teaspoon crushed red pepper
- 4 chicken thighs, trimmed
- Kosher salt, to taste

Directions:

1. Rub the chicken thighs with salt, oil, red pepper, garlic, sage, rosemary, lemon zest and juice.
2. Place the chicken in a bowl, cover and marinate for 1 hour for marination.
3. Turn the "Selector" knob to the "Grill Panini" side.
4. Preheat the bottom grill of Presto Electric Griddle at 350 degrees F and the upper grill plate on medium heat.
5. Once it is preheated, open the lid and place 2 chicken thighs in the Griddler.
6. Close the griddler's lid and grill the chicken for 6 minutes.
7. Transfer them to a plate and grill the remaining thighs.
8. Serve warm.

Nutrition Info: (Per Serving): Calories 388 ;Total Fat 8 g ;Saturated Fat 1 g ;Cholesterol 153mg ;sodium 339 mg ;Total Carbs 8 g ;Fiber 1 g ;Sugar 2 g ;Protein 13 g

Whiskey Wings

Servings: 4

Cooking Time: 6 Minutes

Ingredients:

- 1 tbsp Whiskey
- 1/2 tbsp Chili Powder
- 1 tsp Paprika
- 20 Chicken Wings
- ¼ tsp Garlic Powder
- Salt and Pepper, to taste
- 2 tsp Brown Sugar

Directions:

1. Preheat your grill to 375 degrees F.
2. In the meantime, dump all of the ingredients in a large bowl.
3. With your hands, mix well, to coat the chicken wings completely.
4. When the green light is on, open the grill and arrange the chicken wings onto it.
5. Lower the lid and cook closed for 6 minutes. You can check near the end to see if you need to increase (or decrease) the grilling time for your preferred doneness.
6. Serve with rice and enjoy!

Nutrition Info: Calories 210 ;Total Fats 21g ;Carbs 9.3g ;Protein 18g ;Fiber: 0g

Glazed Chicken Drumsticks

Servings: 12
Cooking Time: 25 Minutes

Ingredients:

- 1 (10-ounce) jar red jalapeño pepper jelly
- ¼ cup fresh lime juice
- 12 (6-ounce) chicken drumsticks
- Salt and ground black pepper, as required

Directions:

1. In a small saucepan, add jelly and lime juice over medium heat and cook for about 3-5 minutes or until melted.
2. Remove from the heat and set aside.
3. Sprinkle the chicken drumsticks with salt and black pepper.
4. Place the water tray in the bottom of Presto Electric Griddle.
5. Place about 2 cups of lukewarm water into the water tray.
6. Place the drip pan over water tray and then arrange the heating element.
7. Now, place the grilling pan over heating element.
8. Plugin the Presto Electric Griddle and press the 'Power' button to turn it on.
9. Then press 'Fan" button.
10. Set the temperature settings according to manufacturer's directions.
11. Cover the grill with lid and let it preheat.
12. After preheating, remove the lid and grease the grilling pan.
13. Place the chicken drumsticks over the grilling pan.
14. Cover with the lid and cook for about 15-20 minutes, flipping occasionally.
15. In the last 5 minutes of cooking, baste the chicken thighs with jelly mixture.
16. Serve hot.

Nutrition Info: (Per Serving):Calories 359 ;Total Fat 9.7 g ;Saturated Fat 2.6 g ;Cholesterol 150 mg ;Sodium 155 mg ;Total Carbs 17.1 g ;Fiber 0 g ;Sugar 11.4 g ;Protein 46.8 g

Peach Glazed Chicken Breasts

Servings: 4
Cooking Time: 10 Minutes

Ingredients:

- For Chicken:
- ¼ teaspoon ground cinnamon
- ¼ teaspoon ground nutmeg
- ¼ teaspoon ground cloves
- Salt, as required
- 4 (5-6-ounce) boneless skinless chicken breasts
- For Glaze:
- 1 peach, peeled and pitted
- 1 chipotle in adobo sauce
- 2 tablespoons fresh lemon juice

Directions:

1. In a bowl, place spices and salt and mix well.
2. Rub the chicken breasts with the spice mixture evenly.
3. For glaze: in a food processor, place peach, chipotle and lemon juice and pulse until pureed.
4. Transfer into a bowl and set aside.
5. Place the water tray in the bottom of Presto Electric Griddle.
6. Place about 2 cups of lukewarm water into the water tray.
7. Place the drip pan over water tray and then arrange the heating element.
8. Now, place the grilling pan over heating element.
9. Plugin the Presto Electric Griddle and press the 'Power' button to turn it on.
10. Then press 'Fan" button.
11. Set the temperature settings according to manufacturer's directions.
12. Cover the grill with lid and let it preheat.
13. After preheating, remove the lid and grease the grilling pan.
14. Place the chicken breasts over the grilling pan.
15. Cover with the lid and cook for about 8-10 minutes per side, brushing with the glaze after every 2 minutes.
16. Serve hot.

Nutrition Info: (Per Serving):Calories 287 ;Total Fat 10.7 g ;Saturated Fat 3 g ;Cholesterol 126 mg ;Sodium 163 mg ;Total Carbs 3.9 g ;Fiber 0.8 g ;Sugar 3.7 g ;Protein 41.5 g

Ketchup Glaze Chicken Thighs

Servings: 12

Cooking Time: 16 Minutes

Ingredients:

- ½ cup packed brown sugar
- 1/3 cup ketchup
- 1/3 cup low-sodium soy sauce
- 3 tablespoons sherry
- 1½ teaspoons fresh ginger root, minced
- 1½ teaspoons garlic, minced
- 12 (6-ounce) boneless, skinless chicken thighs

Directions:

1. In a small bowl, place all ingredients except for chicken thighs and mix well.
2. Transfer about 1 1/3 cups for marinade in another bowl and refrigerate.
3. In a zip lock bag, add the remaining marinade and chicken thighs.
4. Seal the bag and shake to coat well.
5. Refrigerate overnight.
6. Remove the chicken thighs from bag and discard the marinade.
7. Place the water tray in the bottom of Presto Electric Griddle.
8. Place about 2 cups of lukewarm water into the water tray.
9. Place the drip pan over water tray and then arrange the heating element.
10. Now, place the grilling pan over heating element.
11. Plugin the Presto Electric Griddle and press the 'Power' button to turn it on.
12. Then press 'Fan" button.
13. Set the temperature settings according to manufacturer's directions.
14. Cover the grill with lid and let it preheat.
15. After preheating, remove the lid and grease the grilling pan.
16. Place the chicken thighs over the grilling pan.
17. Cover with the lid and cook for about 6-8 minutes per side.
18. In the last 5 minutes of cooking, baste the chicken thighs with reserved marinade.
19. Serve hot.

Nutrition Info: (Per Serving):Calories 359 ;Total Fat 12.6 g ;Saturated Fat 3.6 g ;Cholesterol 151 mg ;Sodium 614 mg ;Total Carbs 8.3 g ;Fiber 0 g ;Sugar 7.6 g ;Protein 49.8 g

Yucatan Chicken Skewers

Servings: 6

Cooking Time: 5 Minutes

Ingredients:

- 6 chicken thighs, boneless, cut in half lengthwise
- 1/2 cup orange juice
- 1/4 cup lime juice
- 2 tablespoons canola oil
- 2 tablespoons ancho chile powder
- 3 garlic cloves, chopped
- 2 tablespoons chipotle in adobo sauce, pureed
- Salt and black pepper, to taste

Directions:

1. Mix orange juice, lime juice, canola oil, chile powder, garlic, chipotle, black pepper and salt in a large bowl.
2. Add chicken thighs to the marinade then rub the chicken well.
3. Thread the chicken on the skewers and keep them aside.
4. Turn the "Selector" knob to the "Grill Panini" side.
5. Preheat the bottom grill of Presto Electric Griddle at 350 degrees F and the upper grill plate on medium heat.
6. Once it is preheated, open the lid and place chicken skewers in the Griddler.
7. Close the griddler's lid and grill the chicken for 5 minutes.
8. Serve warm.

Nutrition Info: (Per Serving): Calories 284 ;Total Fat 25 g ;Saturated Fat 1 g ;Cholesterol 49 mg ;Sodium 460 mg ;Total Carbs 35 g ;Fiber 2 g ;Sugar 6 g ;Protein 26g

Grilled Duck Breasts

Servings: 4

Cooking Time: 6 Minutes

Ingredients:

- 1/4 cup olive oil
- 1 tablespoon dried oregano
- 2 pounds duck breasts
- 3 large garlic cloves, grated
- 2 lemons
- Kosher salt and black pepper, to taste

Directions:

1. Rub the duck breast with black pepper, salt, lemon juice, garlic, oregano and olive oil.
2. Place the duck breasts in a plate, cover and marinate for 30 minutes.
3. Turn the "Selector" knob to the "Grill Panini" side.
4. Preheat the bottom grill of Presto Electric Griddle at 350 degrees F and the upper grill plate on medium heat.
5. Once it is preheated, open the lid and place the duck breasts in the Griddler.
6. Close the griddler's lid and grill the duck for 6 minutes.
7. Serve warm.

Nutrition Info: (Per Serving): Calories 301 ;Total Fat 15.8 g ;Saturated Fat 2.7 g ;Cholesterol 75 mg ;Sodium 189 mg ;Total Carbs 31.7 g ;Fiber 0.3 g ;Sugar 0.1 g ;Protein 28.2 g

Teriyaki Chicken Thighs

Servings: 4

Cooking Time: 7 Minutes

Ingredients:

- 4 Chicken Thighs
- ½ cup Brown Sugar
- ½ cup Teriyaki Sauce
- 2 tbsp Rice Vinegar
- 1 thumb-sized piece of Ginger, minced
- ¼ cup Water
- 2 tsp minced Garlic
- 1 tbsp Cornstarch

Directions:

1. Place the sugar, teriyaki sauce, vinegar, ginger, water, and garlic, in a bowl.
2. Mix to combine well.
3. Transfer half of the mixture to a saucepan and set aside.
4. Add the chicken thighs to the bowl, and coat well.
5. Cover the bowl with wrap, and place in the fridge. Let sit for one hour.
6. Preheat your grill to medium.
7. In the meantime, place the saucepan over medium heat and add the cornstarch. Cook until thickened. Remove from heat and set aside.
8. Arrange the thighs onto the preheated bottom and close the lid.
9. Cook for 5 minutes, then open, brush the thickened sauce over, and cover again.
10. Cook for additional minute or two.
11. Serve and enjoy!

Nutrition Info: Calories 321 ;Total Fats 11g ;Carbs 28g ;Protein 31g ;Fiber: 1g

FISH & SEAFOOD RECIPES

Simple Mahi-mahi

Servings: 4
Cooking Time: 10 Minutes

Ingredients:

- 4 (6-ounce) mahi-mahi fillets
- 2 tablespoons olive oil
- Salt and ground black pepper, as required

Directions:

1. Coat fish fillets with olive oil and season with salt and black pepper evenly.
2. Place the water tray in the bottom of Presto Electric Griddle.
3. Place about 2 cups of lukewarm water into the water tray.
4. Place the drip pan over water tray and then arrange the heating element.
5. Now, place the grilling pan over heating element.
6. Plugin the Presto Electric Griddle and press the 'Power' button to turn it on.
7. Then press 'Fan" button.
8. Set the temperature settings according to manufacturer's directions.
9. Cover the grill with lid and let it preheat.
10. After preheating, remove the lid and grease the grilling pan.
11. Place the fish fillets over the grilling pan.
12. Cover with the lid and cook for about 5 minutes per side.
13. Serve hot.

Nutrition Info: (Per Serving):Calories 195 ;Total Fat 7 g ;Saturated Fat 1 g ;Cholesterol 60 mg ;Sodium 182 mg ;Total Carbs 0 g ;Fiber 0 g ;Sugar 0 g ;Protein 31.6 g

Grilled Garlic Scallops

Servings: 4

Cooking Time: 4 Minutes

Ingredients:

- 1/4 cup olive oil
- Juice of 1 lemon
- 3 garlic cloves minced
- 1 tablespoon Italian seasoning
- Salt and black pepper, to taste
- 1-pound scallops

Directions:

1. Mix Italian seasoning, black pepper, salt, garlic cloves, lemon juice and olive oil in a bowl.
2. Toss in scallops, mix gently, cover and refrigerate for 30 minutes.
3. Turn the "Selector" knob to the "Griddle" side.
4. Preheat the bottom grill of Presto Electric Griddle at 350 degrees F.
5. Once it is preheated, open the lid and place the scallops in the Griddler.
6. Grill the scallop for 2 minutes flip and grill for 2 minutes.
7. Serve warm.

Nutrition Info: (Per Serving): Calories 351 ;Total Fat 4 g ;Saturated Fat 6.3 g ;Cholesterol 360 mg ;Sodium 236 mg ;Total Carbs 19.1 g ;Sugar 0.3 g ;Fiber 0.1 g ;Protein 36 g

Barbecue Squid

Servings: 4

Cooking Time: 3 Minutes

Ingredients:

- 1 ½ pounds skinless squid tubes, sliced
- ⅓ cup red bell pepper, chopped
- 13 fresh red Thai chiles, stemmed
- 6 garlic cloves, minced
- 3 shallots, chopped
- 1 (1-inch) piece fresh ginger, chopped
- 6 tablespoons sugar
- 2 tablespoons soy sauce
- 1 ½ teaspoons black pepper
- ¼ teaspoon salt

Directions:

1. Blend bell pepper, red chilies, shallots, sugar, soy sauce, black pepper and salt in a blender.
2. Transfer this marinade to a Ziplock bag and ad squid tubes.
3. Seal the bag and refrigerate for 1 hour for marination.
4. Turn the "Selector" knob to the "Grill Panini" side.
5. Preheat the bottom grill of Presto Electric Griddle at 350 degrees F and the upper grill plate on medium heat.
6. Once it is preheated, open the lid and place the squid chunks in the Griddler.
7. Close the griddler's lid and grill the squid for 2-3 minutes.
8. Serve warm.

Nutrition Info: (Per Serving): Calories 248 ;Total Fat 15.7 g ;Saturated Fat 2.7 g ;Cholesterol 75 mg ;Sodium 94 mg ;Total Carbs 31.4 g ;Fiber 0.4 g ;Sugar 3.1 g ;Protein 24.9 g

Lemony Cod

Servings: 2

Cooking Time: 14 Minutes

Ingredients:

- 1 garlic cloves, minced
- ½ tablespoon fresh olive oil
- 1 tablespoon fresh lemon juice
- ½ teaspoon dried rosemary, crushed
- ¼ teaspoon paprika
- Salt and ground black pepper, as required
- 2 (6-ounce) skinless, boneless cod fillets

Directions:

1. In a large bowl, mix together all ingredients except cod fillets.
2. Add the cod fillets and coat with garlic mixture generously.
3. Place the water tray in the bottom of Presto Electric Griddle.
4. Place about 2 cups of lukewarm water into the water tray.
5. Place the drip pan over water tray and then arrange the heating element.
6. Now, place the grilling pan over heating element.
7. Plugin the Presto Electric Griddle and press the 'Power' button to turn it on.
8. Then press 'Fan" button.
9. Set the temperature settings according to manufacturer's directions.
10. Cover the grill with lid and let it preheat.
11. After preheating, remove the lid and grease the grilling pan.
12. Place the cod fillets over the grilling pan.
13. Cover with the lid and cook for about 6-7 minutes per side.
14. Serve hot.

Nutrition Info: (Per Serving):Calories 173 ;Total Fat 5.2 g ;Saturated Fat 0.6 g ;Cholesterol 84 mg ;Sodium 186 mg ;Total Carbs 1 g ;Fiber 0.3 g ;Sugar 0.2 g ;Protein 30.6 g

Lemony Salmon

Servings: 4
Cooking Time: 14 Minutes

Ingredients:

- 2 garlic cloves, minced
- 1 tablespoon fresh lemon zest, grated
- 2 tablespoons butter, melted
- 2 tablespoons fresh lemon juice
- Salt and ground black pepper, as required
- 4 (6-ounce) boneless, skinless salmon fillets

Directions:

1. In a bowl, place all ingredients (except salmon fillets) and mix well.
2. Add the salmon fillets and coat with garlic mixture generously.
3. Place the water tray in the bottom of Presto Electric Griddle.
4. Place about 2 cups of lukewarm water into the water tray.
5. Place the drip pan over water tray and then arrange the heating element.
6. Now, place the grilling pan over heating element.
7. Plugin the Presto Electric Griddle and press the 'Power' button to turn it on.
8. Then press 'Fan" button.
9. Set the temperature settings according to manufacturer's directions.
10. Cover the grill with lid and let it preheat.
11. After preheating, remove the lid and grease the grilling pan.
12. Place the salmon fillets over the grilling pan.
13. Cover with the lid and cook for about 6-7 minutes per side.
14. Serve immediately.

Nutrition Info: (Per Serving):Calories 281 ;Total Fat 16.3 g ;Saturated Fat 5.2 g ;Cholesterol 90 mg ;Sodium 157 mg ;Total Carbs 1 g ;Fiber 0.2 g ;Sugar 0.3 g ;Protein 33.3 g

Seasoned Tuna

Servings: 2

Cooking Time: 6 Minutes

Ingredients:

- 2 (6-ounce) yellowfin tuna steaks
- 2 tablespoons blackening seasoning
- Olive oil cooking spray

Directions:

1. Coat the tuna steaks with the blackening seasoning evenly.
2. Then spray tuna steaks with cooking spray.
3. Place the water tray in the bottom of Presto Electric Griddle.
4. Place about 2 cups of lukewarm water into the water tray.
5. Place the drip pan over water tray and then arrange the heating element.
6. Now, place the grilling pan over heating element.
7. Plugin the Presto Electric Griddle and press the 'Power' button to turn it on.
8. Then press 'Fan" button.
9. Set the temperature settings according to manufacturer's directions.
10. Cover the grill with lid and let it preheat.
11. After preheating, remove the lid and grease the grilling pan.
12. Place the tuna steaks over the grilling pan.
13. Cover with the lid and cook for about 2-3 minutes per side.
14. Serve hot.

Nutrition Info: (Per Serving):Calories 313 ;Total Fat 10.7 g ;Saturated Fat 2.2 g ;Cholesterol 83 mg ;Sodium 169 mg ;Total Carbs 0 g ;Fiber 0 g ;Sugar 0 g ;Protein 50.9 g

Shrimp Kabobs

Servings: 6
Cooking Time: 8 Minutes

Ingredients:

- 1 jalapeño pepper, chopped
- 1 large garlic clove, chopped
- 1 (1-inch) fresh ginger, mined
- 1/3 cup fresh mint leaves
- 1 cup coconut milk
- ¼ cup fresh lime juice
- 1 tablespoon red boat fish sauce
- 24 medium shrimp, peeled and deveined
- 1 avocado, peeled, pitted and cubed
- 3 cups seedless watermelon, cubed

Directions:

1. In a food processor, add jalapeño, garlic, ginger, mint, coconut milk, lime juice and fish sauce and pulse until smooth.
2. Add shrimp and coat with marinade generously.
3. Cover and refrigerate to marinate for at least 1-2 hours.
4. Remove shrimp from marinade and thread onto pre-soaked wooden skewers with avocado and watermelon.
5. Place the water tray in the bottom of Presto Electric Griddle.
6. Place about 2 cups of lukewarm water into the water tray.
7. Place the drip pan over water tray and then arrange the heating element.
8. Now, place the grilling pan over heating element.
9. Plugin the Presto Electric Griddle and press the 'Power' button to turn it on.
10. Then press 'Fan" button.
11. Set the temperature settings according to manufacturer's directions.
12. Cover the grill with lid and let it preheat.
13. After preheating, remove the lid and grease the grilling pan.
14. Place the skewers over the grilling pan.
15. Cover with the lid and cook for about 3-4 minutes per side.
16. Serve hot.

Nutrition Info: (Per Serving):Calories 294 ;Total Fat 17.7 g ;Saturated Fat 10.4 g ;Cholesterol 185mg ;Sodium 473 mg ;Total Carbs 12.9 g ;Fiber 3.8 g ;Sugar 6.2 g ;Protein 22.9 g;

Shrimp Skewers

Servings: 4

Cooking Time: 4 Minutes

Ingredients:

- 1/3 cup lemon juice
- 2 tablespoons olive oil
- 2 garlic cloves, minced
- 1/2 teaspoon lemon zest, grated
- 1 lb. uncooked shrimp, peeled and deveined
- Salt and black pepper, to taste

Directions:

1. Season the shrimp with olive oil, salt, black pepper lemon juice, lemon zest, oil, and garlic in a suitable bowl.
2. Thread the seasoned shrimp on the skewers.
3. And season the skewers with salt and black pepper.
4. Turn the "Selector" knob to the "Grill Panini" side.
5. Preheat the bottom grill of Presto Electric Griddle at 350 degrees F and the upper grill plate on medium heat.
6. Once it is preheated, open the lid and place the shrimp skewers in the Griddler.
7. Close the griddler's lid and grill the skewers for 4 minutes.
8. Serve warm.

Nutrition Info: (Per Serving): Calories 338 ;Total Fat 3.8 g ;Saturated Fat 0.7 g ;Cholesterol 22 mg ;Sodium 620 mg ;Total Carbs 28.3 g ;Fiber 2.4 g ;Sugar 1.2 g ;Protein 15.4 g

Pistachio Pesto Shrimp

Servings: 4

Cooking Time: 4 Minutes

Ingredients:

- ¾ cup fresh arugula
- ½ cup fresh parsley, minced
- 1/3 cup shelled pistachios
- 2 tablespoons lemon juice
- 1 garlic clove, peeled
- ¼ teaspoon lemon zest, grated
- ½ cup olive oil
- ¼ cup Parmesan cheese, shredded
- ¼ teaspoon salt
- 1/8 teaspoon pepper
- 1 ½ lbs. jumbo shrimp, peeled and deveined

Directions:

1. Start by blending the arugula, parsley, pistachios, lemon juice, garlic, lemon zest, and olive oil in a blender until smooth.
2. Stir in salt, black pepper, Parmesan cheese, and mix well.
3. Toss the shrimp with the prepared sauce in a bowl then cover to refrigerate for 30 minutes.
4. Thread these pesto shrimps on the wooden skewers.
5. Turn the "Selector" knob to the "Grill Panini" side.
6. Preheat the bottom grill of Presto Electric Griddle at 350 degrees F and the upper grill plate on medium heat.
7. Once it is preheated, open the lid and place the pesto skewers in the Griddler.
8. Close the griddler's lid and grill the shrimp skewers for 4 minutes.
9. Serve warm.

Nutrition Info: (Per Serving): Calories 293 ;Total Fat 16 g ;Saturated Fat 2.3 g ;Cholesterol 75 mg ;Sodium 386 mg ;Total Carbs 5.2 g ;Sugar 2.6 g ;Fiber 1.9 g ;Protein 34.2 g

Blackened Tilapia

Servings: 4

Cooking Time: 8 Minutes

Ingredients:

- 4 Tilapia Fillets
- 3 tsp Paprika
- ½ tsp Garlic Powder
- ¼ tsp Onion Powder
- ¼ tsp Black Pepper
- ¾ tsp Salt
- 2 tbsp Olive Oil

Directions:

1. Preheat your grill to 375 degrees F.
2. Place the oil and spices in a small bowl and mix to combine.
3. Rub the mixture into the tilapia fillets, making sure to coat well.
4. When the green light indicates the unit is ready for grilling, arrange the tilapia onto the bottom plate.
5. With the lid off, cook for 4 minutes.
6. Flip over, and thencook for another four minutes. Feel free to increase the cooking time if you like your fish especially burnt.
7. Serve as desired and enjoy!

Nutrition Info: Calories 175 ;Total Fats 9g ;Carbs 1g ;Protein 23.5g ;Fiber: 0.6g

Blackened Salmon

Servings: 2

Cooking Time: 6 Minutes

Ingredients:

- 1 lb. salmon fillets
- 3 tablespoons butter, melted
- 1 tablespoon lemon pepper
- 1 teaspoon seasoned salt
- 1½ tablespoon smoked paprika
- 1 teaspoon cayenne pepper
- ¾ teaspoon onion salt
- ½ teaspoon dry basil
- ½ teaspoon ground white pepper
- ½ teaspoon ground black pepper
- ¼ teaspoon dry oregano
- ¼ teaspoon ancho chili powder

Directions:

1. Liberally season the salmon fillets with butter and other ingredients.
2. Turn the "Selector" knob to the "Grill Panini" side.
3. Preheat the bottom grill of Presto Electric Griddle at 350 degrees F and the upper grill plate on medium heat.
4. Once it is preheated, open the lid and place the salmon fillets in the Griddler.
5. Close the griddler's lid and grill the fish fillets for 6 minutes.
6. Serve warm.

Nutrition Info: (Per Serving): Calories 378 ;Total Fat 7 g ;Saturated Fat 8.1 g ;Cholesterol 230 mg ;Sodium 316 mg ;Total Carbs 16.2 g ;Sugar 0.2 g ;Fiber 0.3 g ;Protein 26 g

Soy Sauce Salmon

Servings: 4
Cooking Time: 10 Minutes

Ingredients:

- 2 tablespoons scallions, chopped
- ¾ teaspoon fresh ginger, minced
- 1 garlic clove, minced
- ½ teaspoon dried dill weed, crushed
- ¼ cup olive oil
- 2 tablespoons balsamic vinegar
- 2 tablespoons low-sodium soy sauce
- 4 (5-ounce) boneless salmon fillets

Directions:

1. Add all ingredients except for salmon in a large bowl and mix well.
2. Add salmon and coat with marinade generously.
3. Cover and refrigerate to marinate for at least 4-5 hours.
4. Place the water tray in the bottom of Presto Electric Griddle.
5. Place about 2 cups of lukewarm water into the water tray.
6. Place the drip pan over water tray and then arrange the heating element.
7. Now, place the grilling pan over heating element.
8. Plugin the Presto Electric Griddle and press the 'Power' button to turn it on.
9. Then press 'Fan" button.
10. Set the temperature settings according to manufacturer's directions.
11. Cover the grill with lid and let it preheat.
12. After preheating, remove the lid and grease the grilling pan.
13. Place the salmon fillets over the grilling pan.
14. Cover with the lid and cook for about 5 minutes per side.
15. Serve hot.

Nutrition Info: (Per Serving):Calories 303 ;Total Fat 21.4 g ;Saturated Fat 3.1 g ;Cholesterol 63 mg ;Sodium 504 mg ;Total Carbs 1.4 g ;Fiber 0.2 g ;Sugar 0.6 g ;Protein 28.2 g

Lemon-garlic Salmon

Servings: 4
Cooking Time: 7 Minutes

Ingredients:

- 2 garlic cloves, minced
- 2 teaspoons lemon zest, grated
- 1/2 teaspoon salt
- 1/2 teaspoon fresh rosemary, minced
- 1/2 teaspoon black pepper
- 4 salmon fillets (6 oz.)

Directions:

1. Mix garlic with lemon zest, salt, rosemary and black pepper in a bowl
2. Leave this spice mixture for 15 minutes then rub it over the salmon with this mixture.
3. Turn the "Selector" knob to the "Grill Panini" side.
4. Preheat the bottom grill of Presto Electric Griddle at 350 degrees F and the upper grill plate on medium heat.
5. Once it is preheated, open the lid and place the salmon in the Griddler.
6. Close the griddler's lid and grill the salmon for 7 minutes.
7. Serve warm.

Nutrition Info: (Per Serving): Calories 246 ;Total Fat 7.4 g ;Saturated Fat 4.6 g ;Cholesterol 105 mg ;Sodium 353 mg ;Total Carbs 19.4 g ;Sugar 6.5 g ;Fiber 2.7 g ;Protein 37.2 g

Lemon Pepper Salmon With Cherry Tomatoes And Asparagus

Servings: 4

Cooking Time: 5 Minutes

Ingredients:

- 4 Salmon Fillets
- 8 Cherry Tomatoes
- 12 Asparagus Spears
- 2 tbsp Olive Oil
- ½ tsp Garlic Powder
- 1 tsp Lemon Pepper
- ½ tsp Onion Powder
- Salt, to taste

Directions:

1. Preheat your grill to 375 degrees F and cut the tomatoes in half.
2. Brush the salmon, tomatoes, and sparagus with olive oil, and then sprinkle with the spices.
3. Arrange the salmon fillets, cherry tomatoes, and asparagus spears, onto the bottom plate.
4. Gently, lower the lid, and cook the fish and veggies for about 5-6 minutes, or until you reach your desired doneness (check at the 5th minute).
5. Serve and enjoy!

Nutrition Info: Calories 240 ;Total Fats 14g ;Carbs 3.5g ;Protein 24g ;Fiber: 1.4g

Lime Sea Bass

Servings: 4
Cooking Time: 9 Minutes

Ingredients:

- ½ tsp Garlic Powder
- 4 tbsp Lime Juice
- 4 Sea Bass Fillets
- Salt and Pepper, to taste

Directions:

1. Preheat your grill to 375 degrees F.
2. Brush the fillets with lime juice and sprinkle with garlic powder, salt, and pepper.
3. When the green light is on, open the grill, coat with cooking spray, and arrange the fillets on top.
4. Cook open for 4 minutes. Then flip over and cook for 4-5 more minutes on the other side.
5. Serve with rice or favorite side dish, ad enjoy!

Nutrition Info: Calories 130 ;Total Fats 2.6g ;Carbs 0g ;Protein 24g ;Fiber: 0g

Grilled Scallops

Servings: 4
Cooking Time: 6 Minutes
Ingredients:
- 1-pound Jumbo Scallops
- 1 ½ tbsp Olive Oil
- ½ tsp Garlic Powder
- Salt and Pepper, to taste
- Dressing:
- 1 tbsp chopped Parsley
- 3 tbsp Lemon Juice
- ½ tsp Lemon Zest
- 2 tbsp Olive Oil
- Salt and Pepper, to taste

Directions:
1. Preheat your grill to medium-high.
2. Brush the scallops with olive oi, and sprinkle with salt, pepper, and garlic powder.
3. Arrange onto the bottom plate and cook for about 3 minutes, with the lid off.
4. Flip over, and grill for an additional two or three minutes.
5. Meanwhile, make the dressing by combining all of the ingredients in a small bowl.
6. Transfer the grilled scallops to a serving plate and drizzle the dressing over.
7. Enjoy!

Nutrition Info: Calories 102 ;Total Fats 5g ;Carbs 3g ;Protein 9.5g ;Fiber: 1g

Tuna Steak With Avocado & Mango Salsa

Servings: 2

Cooking Time: 8 Minutes

Ingredients:

- 2 Tuna Steaks
- 1 ½ tbsp Olive Oil
- 1 tsp Paprika
- 2 tbsp Coconut Sugar
- 1 tsp Onion Powder
- ¼ tsp Pepper
- ½ tsp Salt
- 2/3 tsp Cumin
- Salsa:
- 1 Avocado, pitted and diced
- 1 Mango, diced
- 1 tbsp Olive Oil
- 1 tsp Honey
- ½ Red Onion, diced
- 2 tbsp Lime Juice
- Pinch of Salt

Directions:

1. Preheat your grill to 350-375 degrees F.
2. Place the olive oil and spices in a small bowl and rub the tuna steaks with the mixture.
3. Place on top of the bottom plate and cook for 4 minutes.
4. Flip the steaks over and cook for another 4 minutes.
5. Meanwhile, prepare the salsa by placing all of the salsa ingredients in a bowl, and mixing well to combine.
6. Transfer the grilled tuna steaks to two serving plates and divide the avocado and mango salsa among them.
7. Enjoy!

Nutrition Info: Calories 280 ;Total Fats 26g ;Carbs 12g ;Protein 24g ;Fiber: 2g

Salmon Lime Burgers

Servings: 2

Cooking Time: 6 Minutes

Ingredients:

- 1-lb. skinless salmon fillets, minced
- 2 tablespoons grated lime zest
- 1 tablespoon Dijon mustard
- 3 tablespoons shallot, chopped
- 2 tablespoons fresh cilantro, minced
- 1 tablespoon soy sauce
- 1 tablespoon honey
- 3 garlic cloves, minced
- 1/2 teaspoon salt
- 1/4 teaspoon black pepper

Directions:

1. Thoroughly mix all the ingredients for burgers in a bowl.
2. Make four patties out this salmon mixture.
3. Turn the "Selector" knob to the "Grill Panini" side.
4. Preheat the bottom grill of Presto Electric Griddle at 350 degrees F and the upper grill plate on medium heat.
5. Once it is preheated, open the lid and place the salmon burgers in the Griddler.
6. Close the griddler's lid and grill the salmon burgers for 6 minutes.
7. Serve warm with buns.

Nutrition Info: (Per Serving): Calories 408 ;Total Fat 21 g ;Saturated Fat 4.3 g ;Cholesterol 150 mg ;Sodium 146 mg ;Total Carbs 21.1 g ;Sugar 0.1 g ;Fiber 0.4 g ;Protein 23 g

The Easiest Pesto Shrimp

Servings: 2

Cooking Time: 5 Minutes

Ingredients:

- 1-pound Shrimp, tails and shells discarded
- ½ cup Pesto Sauce

Directions:

1. Place the cleaned shrimp in a bowl and add the pesto sauce to it.
2. Mix gently with your hands, until each shrimp is coated with the sauce. Let sit for about 15 minutes.
3. In the meantime, preheat your grill to 350 degrees F.
4. Open the grill and arrange the shrimp onto the bottom plate.
5. Cook with the lid off for about 2-3 minutes. Flip over and cook for an additional 2 minutes.
6. Serve as desired and enjoy!

Nutrition Info: Calories 470 ;Total Fats 28.5g ;Carbs 3g ;Protein 50g ;Fiber: 0g

Orange-glazed Salmon

Servings: 4

Cooking Time: 8 Minutes

Ingredients:

- 4 Salmon Fillets
- ½ tsp Garlic Powder
- 1 tsp Paprika
- ¼ tsp Cayenne Pepper
- 1 ¾ tsp Salt
- 1 tbsp Brown Sugar
- ¼ tsp Black Pepper
- Glaze:
- 1 tsp Salt
- 2 tbsp Soy Sauce
- Juice of 1 Orange
- 4 tbsp Maple Syrup

Directions:

1. Preheat your grill to medium and coat with cooking spray.
2. In a small bowl, combine the spices together, and then massage the mixture into the fish.
3. Arrange the salmon onto the bottom plate and cook with the lid off.
4. In the meantime, place the glaze ingredients in a saucepan over medium heat.
5. Cook for a couple of minutes, until thickened.
6. Once the salmon has been cooking for 3 minutes, flip it over.
7. Cook for another 3 minutes.
8. Then, brush with the glaze, lower the lid, and cook for an additional minute.
9. Serve with preferred side dish. Enjoy!

Nutrition Info: Calories 250 ;Total Fats 19g ;Carbs 7g ;Protein 22g ;Fiber: 0g

Buttered Halibut

Servings: 2

Cooking Time: 8 Minutes

Ingredients:

- 2 (4-ounce) haddock fillets
- Salt and ground black pepper, as required
- 1 tablespoon butter, melted

Directions:

1. Sprinkle the fish fillets with salt and black pepper generously.
2. Place the water tray in the bottom of Presto Electric Griddle.
3. Place about 2 cups of lukewarm water into the water tray.
4. Place the drip pan over water tray and then arrange the heating element.
5. Now, place the grilling pan over heating element.
6. Plugin the Presto Electric Griddle and press the 'Power' button to turn it on.
7. Then press 'Fan" button.
8. Set the temperature settings according to manufacturer's directions.
9. Cover the grill with lid and let it preheat.
10. After preheating, remove the lid and grease the grilling pan.
11. Place the fish fillets over the grilling pan.
12. Cover with the lid and cook for about 3-4 minutes per side.
13. Remove from the grill and place the haddock fillets onto serving plates.
14. Drizzle with melted butter and serve.

Nutrition Info: (Per Serving):Calories 178 ;Total Fat 6.8 g ;Saturated Fat 3.8 g ;Cholesterol 99 mg ;Sodium 217 mg ;Total Carbs 0 g ;Fiber 0 g ;Sugar 0 g ;Protein 27.6 g

Herbed Salmon

Servings: 4
Cooking Time: 8 Minutes

Ingredients:

- 2 garlic cloves, minced
- 1 teaspoon dried oregano, crushed
- 1 teaspoon dried basil, crushed
- Salt and ground black pepper, as required
- ¼ cup olive oil
- 2 tablespoons fresh lemon juice
- 4 (4-ounce) salmon fillets

Directions:

1. In a large bowl, add all ingredients except for salmon and mix well.
2. Add the salmon and coat with marinade generously.
3. Cover and refrigerate to marinate for at least 1 hour.
4. Place the water tray in the bottom of Presto Electric Griddle.
5. Place about 2 cups of lukewarm water into the water tray.
6. Place the drip pan over water tray and then arrange the heating element.
7. Now, place the grilling pan over heating element.
8. Plugin the Presto Electric Griddle and press the 'Power' button to turn it on.
9. Then press 'Fan" button.
10. Set the temperature settings according to manufacturer's directions.
11. Cover the grill with lid and let it preheat.
12. After preheating, remove the lid and grease the grilling pan.
13. Place the salmon fillets over the grilling pan.
14. Cover with the lid and cook for about 4 minutes per side.
15. Serve hot.

Nutrition Info: (Per Serving):Calories 263 ;Total Fat 19.7 g ;Saturated Fat 2.9 g ;Cholesterol 50 mg ;Sodium 91 mg ;Total Carbs 0.9 g ;Fiber 0.2 g ;Sugar 0.2 g ;Protein 22.2 g

Ginger Salmon

Servings: 3
Cooking Time: 8 Minutes

Ingredients:

- Sauce:
- ¼ tablespoons rice vinegar
- 1 teaspoons sugar
- 1/8 teaspoon salt
- ¼ tablespoon lime zest, grated
- 1/8 cup lime juice
- ½ tablespoon olive oil
- 1/8 teaspoon ground coriander
- 1/8 teaspoon ground black pepper
- 1/8 cup cilantro, chopped
- ¼ tablespoon onion, chopped
- ½ teaspoon ginger root, minced
- 1 garlic clove, minced
- 1 small cucumber, peeled, chopped
- Salmon:
- 2 tablespoons gingerroot, minced
- ¼ tablespoon lime juice
- ¼ tablespoon olive oil
- Salt, to taste
- Black pepper, to taste
- 3 (6 oz.) salmon fillets

Directions:

1. Start by blending the cucumber with all the sauce ingredients in a blender until smooth.
2. Season and rub the salmon fillets with ginger, oil, salt, black pepper, lime juice.
3. Turn the "Selector" knob to the "Grill Panini" side.
4. Preheat the bottom grill of Presto Electric Griddle at 350 degrees F and the upper grill plate on medium heat.
5. Once it is preheated, open the lid and place the salmon fillets in the Griddler.
6. Close the griddler's lid and grill the salmon fillets for 8 minutes.
7. Serve warm with cucumber sauce.

Nutrition Info: (Per Serving): Calories 457 ;Total Fat 19.1 g ;Saturated Fat 11 g ;Cholesterol 262 mg ;Sodium 557 mg ;Total Carbs 18.9 g ;Sugar 1.2 g ;Fiber 1.7 g ;Protein 32.5 g

BEEF, PORK & LAMB RECIPES

Hawaian Kebobs

Servings: 4
Cooking Time: 6 Minutes
Ingredients:
- ½ cup Orange Juice
- 1 tbsp minced Garlic
- 1/3 cup Brown Sugar
- ½ tbs minced Ginger
- ½ cup Soy Sauce
- 1-pound Top Sirloin
- 1-pound Pineapple, fresh
- 2 Bell Peppers
- ½ Red Onion

Directions:
1. Place the first 5 ingredients in a medium bowl. Whisk to combine well.
2. Cut the steak into pieces and add to the bowl.
3. Stir well to coat, cover with plastic wrap, and place in the fridge for at least 60 minutes.
4. Meanwhile, cut the red onion, pineapple, and bell pepper, into chunks.
5. If using wooden skewers, soak them in cold water.
6. Preheat your grill to medium-high.
7. Thread the steak, pineapple, onion, and bell peppers onto the skewers.
8. Open the grill and arrange the skewers onto the bottom plate.
9. Cover, and let cook for 6 minutes.
10. Serve and enjoy!

Nutrition Info: Calories 460 ;Total Fats 13g ;Carbs 51g ;Protein 33g ;Fiber: 0.7g

Fajita Skewers

Servings: 6

Cooking Time: 7 Minutes

Ingredients:

- 1 lb. sirloin steak, cubed
- 1 bunch scallions, cut into large pieces
- 1 pack flour tortillas, cut into triangles
- 4 large bell peppers, cubed
- olive oil, for drizzling
- Salt to taste
- Black pepper to taste

Directions:

1. Thread the steak, tortillas, peppers, and scallions on the skewers.
2. Drizzle salt, black pepper, and olive oil over the skewers.
3. Turn the "Selector" knob to the "Grill Panini" side.
4. Preheat the bottom grill of Presto Electric Griddle at 350 degrees F and the upper grill plate on medium heat.
5. Once it is preheated, open the lid and place the fajita skewers in the Griddler.
6. Close the griddler's lid and grill the skewers for 7 minutes.
7. Serve warm.

Nutrition Info: (Per Serving): Calories 353 ;Total Fat 7.5 g ;Saturated Fat 1.1 g ;Cholesterol 20 mg ;Sodium 297 mg ;Total Carbs 10.4 g ;Fiber 0.2 g ;Sugar 0.1 g ;Protein 13.1 g

Glazed Pork Chops

Servings: 6

Cooking Time: 12 Minutes

Ingredients:

- 2 tablespoons fresh ginger root, minced
- 1 teaspoon garlic, minced
- 2 tablespoons fresh orange zest, grated finely
- ½ cup fresh orange juice
- 1 teaspoon garlic chile paste
- 2 tablespoons soy sauce
- Salt, as required
- 6 (½-inch thick) pork loin chops

Directions:

1. In a large bowl, mix together all ingredients except for chops.
2. Add chops and coat with marinade generously.
3. Cover and refrigerate to marinate for about 2 hours, tossing occasionally.
4. Place the water tray in the bottom of Presto Electric Griddle.
5. Place about 2 cups of lukewarm water into the water tray.
6. Place the drip pan over water tray and then arrange the heating element.
7. Now, place the grilling pan over heating element.
8. Plugin the Presto Electric Griddle and press the 'Power' button to turn it on.
9. Then press 'Fan" button.
10. Set the temperature settings according to manufacturer's directions.
11. Cover the grill with lid and let it preheat.
12. After preheating, remove the lid and grease the grilling pan.
13. Place the chops over the grilling pan.
14. Cover with the lid and cook for about 10-12 minutes, flipping once in the middle way or until desired doneness.
15. Serve hot.

Nutrition Info: (Per Serving):Calories 560 ;Total Fat 42.3 g ;Saturated Fat 15.9 g ;Cholesterol 146 mg ;Sodium 447 mg ;Total Carbs 3.5 g ;Fiber 0.3 g ;Sugar 1.9 g ;Protein 38.8 g

Rosemary Lamb Chops

Servings: 2

Cooking Time: 10 Minutes

Ingredients:

- 1 tablespoon olive oil
- 1 tablespoon fresh lemon juice
- 1 tablespoon fresh rosemary, chopped
- ½ teaspoon garlic, minced
- Salt and ground black pepper, as required
- 2 (8-ounce) (½-inch-thick) lamb shoulder blade chops

Directions:

1. In a bowl, place all ingredients and beat until well combined.
2. Place the chops and oat with the mixture well.
3. Seal the bag and shake vigorously to coat evenly.
4. Place the water tray in the bottom of Presto Electric Griddle.
5. Place about 2 cups of lukewarm water into the water tray.
6. Place the drip pan over water tray and then arrange the heating element.
7. Now, place the grilling pan over heating element.
8. Plugin the Presto Electric Griddle and press the 'Power' button to turn it on.
9. Then press 'Fan" button.
10. Set the temperature settings according to manufacturer's directions.
11. Cover the grill with lid and let it preheat.
12. After preheating, remove the lid and grease the grilling pan.
13. Place the lamb chops over the grilling pan.
14. Cover with the lid and cook for about 4-5 minutes per side.
15. Serve hot.

Nutrition Info: (Per Serving):Calories 410 ;Total Fat 25.4 g ;Saturated Fat 7.2 g ;Cholesterol 151 mg ;Sodium 241 mg ;Total Carbs 1.5 g ;Fiber 0.7 g ;Sugar 0.2 g ;Protein 44.3 g

Teriyaki Beef Skewers

Servings: 6
Cooking Time: 6 Minutes

Ingredients:

- ¾ cup brown sugar
- ¼ cup soy sauce
- 1/8 cup pineapple juice
- 1/8 cup water
- 2 tablespoons vegetable oil
- 1 garlic clove, chopped
- 2 pounds boneless round steak, sliced

Directions:

1. Mix brown sugar, soy sauce, pineapple juice, water, vegetable oi, garlic cloves and steak slices in a bowl.
2. Cover and refrigerate the steaks for 24 hours for marination.
3. Thread the marinated beef on the wooden skewers.
4. Turn the "Selector" knob to the "Grill Panini" side.
5. Preheat the bottom grill of Presto Electric Griddle at 350 degrees F and the upper grill plate on medium heat.
6. Once it is preheated, open the lid and place the skewers in the Griddler.
7. Close the griddler's lid and grill the skewers for 6 minutes.
8. Serve warm.

Nutrition Info: (Per Serving): Calories 380 ;Total Fat 20 g ;Saturated Fat 5 g ;Cholesterol 151 mg ;Sodium 686 mg ;Total Carbs 33 g ;Fiber 1 g ;Sugar 1.2 g ;Protein 21 g

Grilled Lamb With Herbes De Provence

Servings: 6

Cooking Time: 18 Minutes

Ingredients:

- 1 rib (3 ounces-1-inch-thick) lamb chops
- 1/4 cups olive oil
- 2 lemons, juiced
- Salt and black pepper, to taste
- 3 tablespoons Herbes de Provence

Directions:

1. Rub the lamb chops with lemon juice, olive oil, black pepper, salt and Herbes de Provence.
2. Cover and marinate the chops for 1 hour in the refrigerator.
3. Turn the "Selector" knob to the "Grill Panini" side.
4. Preheat the bottom grill of Presto Electric Griddle at 350 degrees F and the upper grill plate on medium heat.
5. Once it is preheated, open the lid and place half of the chops in the Griddler.
6. Close the griddler's lid and grill the chops for 9 minutes.
7. Transfer the grilled chops to a plate and grill the remaining chops in the same manner.
8. Serve warm.

Nutrition Info: (Per Serving): Calories 308 ;Total Fat 20.5 g ;Saturated Fat 3 g ;Cholesterol 42 mg ;Sodium 688 mg ;Total Carbs 40.3 g ;Sugar 1.4 g ;Fiber 4.3 g ;Protein 49 g

Maple Pork Chops

Servings: 1
Cooking Time: 7-8 Minutes

Ingredients:

- 4 boneless Pork Chops
- 6 tbsp Balsamic Vinegar
- 6 tbsp Maple Syrup
- ¼ tsp ground Sage
- Salt and Pepper, to taste

Directions:

1. Whisk the vinegar, maple, sage, and some salt and pepper in a bowl.
2. Add the pork chops and coat well.
3. Cover with plastic foil and refrigerate for one hour.
4. Preheat your grill to 350 degrees F.
5. Open and arrange the chops onto the bottom plate.
6. Lower the lid and cook closed for about 7 minutes, or until your desired doneness is reached.
7. Serve and enjoy!

Nutrition Info: Calories 509 ;Total Fats 19g ;Carbs 15g ;Protein 65g ;Fiber: 0g

Spiced Pork Tenderloin

Servings: 6
Cooking Time: 18 Minutes

Ingredients:

- 2 teaspoons fennel seeds
- 2 teaspoons coriander seeds
- 2 teaspoons caraway seeds
- 1 teaspoon cumin seeds
- 1 bay leaf
- Salt and freshly ground black pepper, to taste
- 2 tablespoons fresh dill, chopped
- 2 (1-pound) pork tenderloins, trimmed

Directions:

1. For spice rub: in a spice grinder, add the seeds and bay leaf and grind until finely powdered.
2. Add the salt and black pepper and mix.
3. In a small bowl, reserve 2 tablespoons of spice rub.
4. In another small bowl, mix together the remaining spice rub, and dill.
5. Place 1 tenderloin onto a piece of plastic wrap.
6. With a sharp knife, slice through the meat to within ½-inch of the opposite side. Now, open the tenderloin like a book.
7. Cover with another plastic wrap and with a meat pounder, gently pound into ½-inch thickness.
8. Repeat with the remaining tenderloin.
9. Remove the plastic wrap and spread half of the spice and dill mixture over the center of each tenderloin.
10. Roll each tenderloin like a cylinder.
11. With a kitchen string, tightly tie each roll at several places.
12. Rub each roll with the reserved spice rub generously.
13. With 1 plastic wrap, wrap each roll and refrigerate for at least 4-6 hours.
14. Place the water tray in the bottom of Presto Electric Griddle.
15. Place about 2 cups of lukewarm water into the water tray.
16. Place the drip pan over water tray and then arrange the heating element.
17. Now, place the grilling pan over heating element.
18. Plugin the Presto Electric Griddle and press the 'Power' button to turn it on.
19. Then press 'Fan" button.
20. Set the temperature settings according to manufacturer's directions.
21. Cover the grill with lid and let it preheat.
22. After preheating, remove the lid and grease the grilling pan.
23. Remove the plastic wrap from tenderloins.
24. Place the tenderloins over the grilling pan.
25. Cover with the lid and cook for about 14-18 minutes, flipping occasionally.
26. Remove from the grill and place tenderloins onto a cutting board.
27. With a piece of foil, cover each tenderloin for at least 5-10 minutes before slicing.
28. With a sharp knife, cut the tenderloins into desired size slices and serve.

Nutrition Info: (Per Serving):Calories 313 ;Total Fat 12.6 g ;Saturated Fat 4.4 g ;Cholesterol 142 mg ;Sodium 127 mg ;Total Carbs 1.4 g ;Fiber 0.7 g ;Sugar 0 g ;Protein 45.7 g

Lamb Steak

Servings: 6

Cooking Time: 4 Minutes

Ingredients:

- 2 garlic cloves, minced
- 2 tablespoons olive oil
- 2 teaspoons dried oregano, crushed
- 2 tablespoons sumac
- 2 teaspoons sweet paprika
- 12 lamb cutlets, trimmed

Directions:

1. In a bowl mix together all ingredients except for lamb cutlets.
2. Add the cutlets and coat with garlic mixture evenly.
3. Set aside for at least 10 minutes.
4. Place the water tray in the bottom of Presto Electric Griddle.
5. Place about 2 cups of lukewarm water into the water tray.
6. Place the drip pan over water tray and then arrange the heating element.
7. Now, place the grilling pan over heating element.
8. Plugin the Presto Electric Griddle and press the 'Power' button to turn it on.
9. Then press 'Fan" button.
10. Set the temperature settings according to manufacturer's directions.
11. Cover the grill with lid and let it preheat.
12. After preheating, remove the lid and grease the grilling pan.
13. Place the cutlets over the grilling pan.
14. Cover with the lid and cook for about 2 minutes from both sides or until desired doneness.
15. Serve hot.

Nutrition Info: (Per Serving):Calories 343 ;Total Fat 16.6 g ;Saturated Fat 4.9 g ;Cholesterol 144 mg ;Sodium 122 mg ;Total Carbs 1 g ;Fiber 0.5 g ;Sugar 0.1 g ;Protein 45.2 g

Chimichurri Beef Skewers

Servings: 6
Cooking Time: 8 Minutes
Ingredients:

- 1/3 cup fresh basil
- 1/3 cup fresh cilantro
- 1/3 cup fresh parsley
- 1 tablespoon red wine vinegar
- Juice of 1/2 lemon
- 1 garlic clove, minced
- 1 shallot, minced
- 1/2 teaspoon crushed red pepper flakes
- 1/2 cup olive oil, divided
- Salt to taste
- Black pepper to taste
- 1 red onion, cubed
- 1 red pepper, cubed
- 1 orange pepper, cubed
- 1 yellow pepper, cubed
- 1 1/2 lb. sirloin steak, fat trimmed and diced

Directions:

1. First, take basil, parsley, vinegar, lemon juice, red pepper, shallots, garlic, and cilantro in a blender jug.
2. Blend well, then add ¼ cup olive oil, salt, and pepper and mix again.
3. Now thread the steak, bell peppers, and onion, alternately on the skewers.
4. Drizzle salt, black pepper, and remaining oil over the skewers.
5. Turn the "Selector" knob to the "Grill Panini" side.
6. Preheat the bottom grill of Presto Electric Griddle at 350 degrees F and the upper grill plate on medium heat.
7. Once it is preheated, open the lid and place the skewers in the Griddler.
8. Close the griddler's lid and grill the skewers for 8 minutes.
9. Serve warm with green sauce.

Nutrition Info: (Per Serving): Calories 231 ;Total Fat 20.1 g ;Saturated Fat 2.4 g ;Cholesterol 110 mg ;Sodium 941 mg ;Total Carbs 20.1 g ;Fiber 0.9 g ;Sugar 1.4 g ;Protein 14.6 g

American Burger

Servings: 4

Cooking Time: 9 Minutes

Ingredients:

- 1/2 cup seasoned bread crumbs
- 1 large egg, lightly beaten
- 1/2 teaspoon salt
- 1/2 teaspoon pepper
- 1-lb. ground beef
- 1 tablespoon olive oil

Directions:

1. Take all the ingredients for a burger in a suitable bowl except the oil and the buns.
2. Mix them thoroughly together and make 4 of the ½ inch patties.
3. Brush these patties with olive oil.
4. Turn the "Selector" knob to the "Grill Panini" side.
5. Preheat the bottom grill of Presto Electric Griddle at 350 degrees F and the upper grill plate on medium heat.
6. Once it is preheated, open the lid and place the patties in the Griddler.
7. Close the griddler's lid and grill the patties for 7-9 minutes.
8. Serve warm.

Nutrition Info: (Per Serving): Calories 301 ;Total Fat 15.8 g ;Saturated Fat 2.7 g ;Cholesterol 75 mg ;Sodium 389 mg ;Total Carbs 11.7 g ;Fiber 0.3g ;Sugar 0.1 g ;Protein 28.2 g

Raspberry Pork Chops

Servings: 4

Cooking Time: 20 Minutes

Ingredients:

- 1/2 cup raspberry preserves
- 1 chipotle in adobo sauce, chopped
- 1/2 teaspoon salt
- 4 bone-in pork loin chops

Directions:

1. Take a small pan and mix preserves with chipotle pepper sauce on medium heat.
2. Keep ¼ cup of this sauce aside and rub the remaining over the pork.
3. Sprinkle salt over the pork and mix well.
4. Turn the "Selector" knob to the "Grill Panini" side.
5. Preheat the bottom grill of Presto Electric Griddle at 350 degrees F and the upper grill plate on medium heat.
6. Once it is preheated, open the lid and place 2 pork chops in the Griddler.
7. Close the griddler's lid and grill the chops for 10 minutes.
8. Transfer them to a serving plate and grill remaining chops in the same manner.
9. Pour the reserved sauce over the pork chops.
10. Serve warm.

Nutrition Info: (Per Serving): Calories 401 ;Total Fat 50.5 g ;Saturated Fat 11.7 g ;Cholesterol 58 mg ;Sodium 463 mg ;Total Carbs 9.9 g ;Fiber 1.5 g ;Sugar 0.3 g ;Protein 29.3 g

Steak Skewers With Potatoes And Mushrooms

Servings: 6

Cooking Time: 10 Minutes

Ingredients:

- 1-pound Steak
- 4 tbsp Olive Oil
- ½ pound Button Mushrooms
- 4 tbsp Balsamic Vinegar
- 1 pound Very Small Potatoes, boiled
- 2 tsp minced Garlic
- ½ tsp dired Sage
- Salt and Pepper, to taste

Directions:

1. Start by cutting the steak into 1-inch pieces.
2. Quarter the mushrooms.
3. Whisk the vinegar, oil, garlic, sage, and salt and pepper, in a bowl.
4. Add the meat, murshooms and potatoes to the bowl, coat well, and place in the fridge for 30 minutes. If your potatoes are not small enough for the skewers, you can chop them into smaller chunks.
5. In the meantime, soak the skewers in cold water.
6. Meanwhile, preheat your grill to medium-high.
7. Thread the chunks onto the skewers and arrange them on the bottom plate.
8. Keep the lid open and cook for 5.
9. Flip over and cook for 5 more minutes.
10. Serve and enjoy!

Nutrition Info: Calories 383 ;Total Fats 23g ;Carbs 21g ;Protein 23g ;Fiber: 3g

Prosciutto-wrapped Pork Chops

Servings: 4

Cooking Time: 14 Minutes

Ingredients:

- 4 (6-ounce) boneless pork chops
- Salt and ground black pepper, as required
- 8 fresh sage leaves
- 8 thin prosciutto slices
- 2 tablespoons olive oil

Directions:

1. Season the pork chops with salt and black pepper evenly.
2. Arrange 2 sage leaves over each pork chop.
3. Wrap each pork chop with 2 prosciutto slices.
4. Lightly brush both sides of chops with olive oil.
5. Place the water tray in the bottom of Presto Electric Griddle.
6. Place about 2 cups of lukewarm water into the water tray.
7. Place the drip pan over water tray and then arrange the heating element.
8. Now, place the grilling pan over heating element.
9. Plugin the Presto Electric Griddle and press the 'Power' button to turn it on.
10. Then press 'Fan" button.
11. Set the temperature settings according to manufacturer's directions.
12. Cover the grill with lid and let it preheat.
13. After preheating, remove the lid and grease the grilling pan.
14. Place the chops over the grilling pan.
15. Cover with the lid and cook for about 6-7 minutes per side.
16. Serves hot.

Nutrition Info: (Per Serving):Calories 384 ;Total Fat 16.1 g ;Saturated Fat 4.1 g ;Cholesterol 154 mg ;Sodium 809 mg ;Total Carbs 0.8 g ;Fiber 0 g ;Sugar 0 g ;Protein 56.2 g

Herbed Lemony Pork Skewers

Servings: 4

Cooking Time: 8 Minutes

Ingredients:

- 1-pound Pork Shoulder or Neck
- 1 tsp dried Basil
- 1 tsp dried Parsley
- 1 tsp dried Oregano
- 2 Garlic Cloves, minced
- 4 tbsp Lemon Juice
- ¼ tsp Onion Powder
- Salt and Pepper, to taste

Directions:

1. Start by soaking 8 skewers in cold water, to prevent the wood from burning on the grill.
2. Cut the pork into small chunks and place in a bowl.
3. Add lemon juice, garlic, spices and herbs to the bowl.
4. Give the mixture a good stir so that the meat is coated well.
5. Preheat your grill to medium-high.
6. Meanwhile, thread the meat onto the skewers.
7. When the green light turns on, arrange the skewers onto the bottom plate.
8. Cook for about 4 minutes per side (or more if you like the meat well-done and almost burnt).
9. Serve as desired and enjoy!

Nutrition Info: Calories 364 ;Total Fats 27g ;Carbs 1.6g ;Protein 26.7g ;Fiber: 0.1g

Spicy Pork Chops

Servings: 4

Cooking Time: 15 Minutes

Ingredients:

- 2 teaspoons Worcestershire sauce
- 1 teaspoon liquid smoke flavoring
- 1 tablespoon onion powder
- 1 tablespoon garlic powder
- 1 tablespoon paprika
- 1 tablespoon seasoned salt
- 1 teaspoon freshly ground black pepper
- 4 (½-¾-inch thick) bone-in pork chops

Directions:

1. In a bowl, mix together all ingredients except for chops.
2. Add chops and coat with mixture generously.
3. Set aside for about 10-15 minutes.
4. Place the water tray in the bottom of Presto Electric Griddle.
5. Place about 2 cups of lukewarm water into the water tray.
6. Place the drip pan over water tray and then arrange the heating element.
7. Now, place the grilling pan over heating element.
8. Plugin the Presto Electric Griddle and press the 'Power' button to turn it on.
9. Then press 'Fan" button.
10. Set the temperature settings according to manufacturer's directions.
11. Cover the grill with lid and let it preheat.
12. After preheating, remove the lid and grease the grilling pan.
13. Place the chops over the grilling pan.
14. Cover with the lid and cook for about 15 minutes, flipping once halfway through.
15. Serve hot.

Nutrition Info: (Per Serving):Calories 262 ;Total Fat 12.3 g ;Saturated Fat 4.1 g ;Cholesterol 85 mg ;Sodium 1800 mg ;Total Carbs 5.7 g ;Fiber 1.1 g ;Sugar 2.8 g ;Protein 29.9 g

Garlicy Lamb Chops

Servings: 4
Cooking Time: 6 Minutes

Ingredients:

- 1 tablespoon fresh ginger, grated
- 4 garlic cloves, chopped roughly
- 1 teaspoon ground cumin
- ½ teaspoon red chili powder
- Salt and ground black pepper, as required
- 1 tablespoon olive oil
- 1 tablespoon fresh lemon juice
- 8 lamb chops, trimmed

Directions:

1. In a bowl, mix together all ingredients except for chops.
2. With a hand blender, blend until a smooth mixture forms.
3. Add the chops and coat with mixture generously.
4. Refrigerate to marinate for overnight.
5. Place the water tray in the bottom of Presto Electric Griddle.
6. Place about 2 cups of lukewarm water into the water tray.
7. Place the drip pan over water tray and then arrange the heating element.
8. Now, place the grilling pan over heating element.
9. Plugin the Presto Electric Griddle and press the 'Power' button to turn it on.
10. Then press 'Fan" button.
11. Set the temperature settings according to manufacturer's directions.
12. Cover the grill with lid and let it preheat.
13. After preheating, remove the lid and grease the grilling pan.
14. Place the lamb chops over the grilling pan.
15. Cover with the lid and cook for about 3 minutes per side.
16. Serve hot.

Nutrition Info: (Per Serving):Calories 465 ;Total Fat 20.4 g ;Saturated Fat 6.5 g ;Cholesterol 204 mg ;Sodium 178 mg ;Total Carbs 2.4 g ;Fiber 0.4 g ;Sugar 0.2 g ;Protein 64.2 g

Beef Skewers

Servings: 6
Cooking Time: 8 Minutes

Ingredients:

- 3 garlic cloves, minced
- 1 tablespoon fresh lemon zest, grated
- 2 teaspoons fresh rosemary, minced
- 2 teaspoons fresh parsley, minced
- 2 teaspoons fresh oregano, minced
- 2 teaspoons fresh thyme, minced
- 4 tablespoons olive oil
- 2 tablespoons fresh lemon juice
- Salt and ground black pepper, as required
- 2 pounds beef sirloin, cut into cubes

Directions:

1. In a bowl, add all the ingredients except the beef and mix well.
2. Add the beef and coat with the herb mixture generously.
3. Refrigerate to marinate for at least 20-30 minutes.
4. Remove the beef cubes from the marinade and thread onto metal skewers.
5. Place the water tray in the bottom of Presto Electric Griddle.
6. Place about 2 cups of lukewarm water into the water tray.
7. Place the drip pan over water tray and then arrange the heating element.
8. Now, place the grilling pan over heating element.
9. Plugin the Presto Electric Griddle and press the 'Power' button to turn it on.
10. Then press 'Fan" button.
11. Set the temperature settings according to manufacturer's directions.
12. Cover the grill with lid and let it preheat.
13. After preheating, remove the lid and grease the grilling pan.
14. Place the skewers over the grilling pan.
15. Cover with the lid and cook for about 6-8 minutes, flipping after every 2 minutes.
16. Remove from the grill and place onto a platter for about 5 minutes before serving.

Nutrition Info: (Per Serving):Calories 369 ;Total Fat 18.9 g ;Saturated Fat 5 g ;Cholesterol 135 mg ;Sodium 129 mg ;Total Carbs 1.6 g ;Fiber 0.6 g ;Sugar 0.2 g ;Protein 46.2 g

Spiced Lamb Chops

Servings: 8

Cooking Time: 8 Minutes

Ingredients:

- 1 tablespoon fresh mint leaves, chopped
- 1 teaspoon garlic paste
- 1 teaspoon ground allspice
- ½ teaspoon ground nutmeg
- ½ teaspoon ground green cardamom
- ¼ teaspoon hot paprika
- Salt and ground black pepper, as required
- 4 tablespoons olive oil
- 2 tablespoons fresh lemon juice
- 2 racks of lamb, trimmed and separated into 16 chops

Directions:

1. In a large bowl, add all the ingredients except for chops and mix until well combined.
2. Add the chops and coat with the mixture generously.
3. Refrigerate to marinate for about 5-6 hours.
4. Place the water tray in the bottom of Presto Electric Griddle.
5. Place about 2 cups of lukewarm water into the water tray.
6. Place the drip pan over water tray and then arrange the heating element.
7. Now, place the grilling pan over heating element.
8. Plugin the Presto Electric Griddle and press the 'Power' button to turn it on.
9. Then press 'Fan" button.
10. Set the temperature settings according to manufacturer's directions.
11. Cover the grill with lid and let it preheat.
12. After preheating, remove the lid and grease the grilling pan.
13. Place the lamb chops over the grilling pan.
14. Cover with the lid and cook for about 6-8 minutes, flipping once halfway through.
15. Serve hot.

Nutrition Info: (Per Serving):Calories 380 ;Total Fat 19.6 g ;Saturated Fat 5.6 g ;Cholesterol 153 mg ;Sodium 150 mg ;Total Carbs 0.5 g ;Fiber 0.2 g ;Sugar 0.1 g ;Protein 47.9 g

Salisbury Steak

Servings: 5

Cooking Time: 12 Minutes

Ingredients:

- 1 1/2 pounds lean ground beef
- 1/2 cup seasoned breadcrumbs
- 1 tablespoon ketchup
- 2 teaspoons dry mustard
- 4 dashes Worcestershire sauce
- 1 cube beef bouillon, crumbled
- Salt and black pepper, to taste
- 1 tablespoon butter, melted

Directions:

1. Mix ground beef with breadcrumbs, ketchup, mustard, Worcestershire sauce, beef bouillon, butter, black pepper and salt in a bowl.
2. Make five patties out of the crumbly beef mixture.
3. Turn the "Selector" knob to the "Grill Panini" side.
4. Preheat the bottom grill of Presto Electric Griddle at 350 degrees F and the upper grill plate on medium heat.
5. Once it is preheated, open the lid and place the patties in the Griddler.
6. Close the griddler's lid and grill the patties for 6 minutes.
7. Serve warm.

Nutrition Info: (Per Serving): Calories 548 ;Total Fat 22.9 g ;Saturated Fat 9 g ;Cholesterol 105 mg ;Sodium 350 mg ;Total Carbs 17.5 g ;Sugar 10.9 g ;Fiber 6.3 g ;Protein 40.1 g

BREADS AND SANDWICHES

The Greatest Butter Burger Recipe

Servings: 6
Cooking Time: 11 Minutes
Ingredients:

- 2 pounds Ground Chuck Meat
- 1 ½ tsp minced Garlic
- 6 tbsp Butter
- 2 tbsp Worcestershire Sauce
- 1 tsp Salt
- ½ tsp Pepper
- 6 Hamburger Buns
- Veggie Toppings of Choice

Directions:

1. Preheat your grill to medium-high.
2. Meanwhile, place the meat, garlic, sauce, salt, and pepper, in a bowl.
3. Mix with your hands to incorporate well. Make six patties out of the mixture.
4. Into each patty, press about one tablespoon into the center.
5. Open the grill and coat with some cooking spray.
6. Arrange the patties onto the bottom plate and cook for 6 minutes.
7. Flip over and cook for 5 more minutes.
8. Serve in hamburger buns with desired veggie toppings.
9. Enjoy!

Nutrition Info: Calories 595 ;Total Fats 48g ;Carbs 25g ;Protein 27g ;Fiber: 1.5g

Simple Pork Chop Sandwich

Servings: 4
Cooking Time: 7 Minutes

Ingredients:

- 4 Hamburger Buns
- 4 Cheddar Slices
- 4 boneless Pork Chop
- Salt and Pepper, to taste
- 4 tbsp Mayonnaise

Directions:

1. Preheat your grill to 375 degrees F.
2. When the green light turns on, open the grill.
3. Season the pork chops with salt and pepper and arrange onto the bottom plate.
4. Lower the lid, and cook the meat closed, for about 5-6 minutes.
5. Open the lid and place a slice of cheddar on top of each chop.
6. Cook for another minute or so, uncovered, until the cheese starts to melt.
7. Spread a tbsp of mayonnaise onto the insides of each bun.
8. Place the cheesy pork chop inside and serve.
9. Enjoy!

Nutrition Info: Calories 510 ;Total Fats 30.6g ;Carbs 18.4g ;Protein 42g ;Fiber: 5g

Chicken Pesto Grilled Sandwich

Servings: 2

Cooking Time: 4 Minutes

Ingredients:

- 4 Slices of Bread
- 1 ½ cups shredded Mozzarella Cheese
- ½ cup Pesto Sauce
- 2 cups cooked and shredded Chicken Meat
- 8 Sundried Tomatoes
- 1 ½ tbsp Butter

Directions:

1. Preheat your grill to medium-high.
2. Combine the pesto and chicken in a bowl.
3. Brush the outsides of the bread with the butter.
4. Divide the pesto/chicken filling between two bread slices.
5. Top with sundried tomatoes and mozzarella cheese.
6. Open the grill and carefully transfer the loaded slices of bread onto the top bottom.
7. Top with the remaining bread slices, carefully.
8. Lower the lid, pressing gently.
9. Let the sandwiches cook for about 3-4 minutes, or until the desired doneness is reached.
10. Serve and enjoy!

Nutrition Info: Calories 725 ;Total Fats 44.5g ;Carbs 32g ;Protein 51g ;Fiber: 7.5g

Fish Tacos With Slaw And Mango Salsa

Servings: 4

Cooking Time: 6 Minutes

Ingredients:

- 4 Tortillas
- 1-pound Cod
- 3 tbsp butter, melted
- ½ tsp Paprika
- ¼ tsp Garlic Onion
- 1 tsp Thyme
- ½ tsp Onion Powder
- ½ tsp Cayenne Pepper
- 1 tsp Brown Sugar
- 1 cup prepared (or store-brought) Slaw
- Salt and Pepper, to taste
- Mango Salsa:
- ¼ cup diced Red Onions
- Juice of 1 Lime
- 1 Mango, diced
- 1 Jalapeno Pepper, deseeded and minced
- 1 tbsp chopped Parlsey or Cilantro

Directions:

1. Preheat your grill to medium.
2. Brush the butter over the cod and sprinkle with the spices.
3. When ready, open the grill, and arrange the cod fillets onto the bottom plate.
4. Lower the lid and cook for about 4-5 minutes in total.
5. Transfer to a plate and cut into chunks.
6. Place all of the mango salsa ingredients in a bowl and mix to combine.
7. Assemble the tacos by adding slaw, topping with grilled cod, and adding a tablespoon or so of the mango salsa.
8. Enjoy!

Nutrition Info: Calories 323 ;Total Fats 12g ;Carbs 31g ;Protein 24g ;Fiber: 3g

Buttery Pepperoni Grilled Cheese Sandwich

Servings: 2

Cooking Time: 5 Minutes

Ingredients:

- 4 slices of Bread
- 4 slices of Mozzarella Cheese
- 4 tbsp Butter
- 18 Pepperoni Slices

Directions:

1. Preheat your grill to medium-high.
2. Meanwhile, brush each slice of bread with a tablespoon of butter. It seems like too much, but the taste is just incredible.
3. Divide the mozzarella and pepperoni among the insides of two bread slices.
4. Top the sandwich with the other slices of bread, keeping the buttery side up.
5. When the green light appears, open the grill.
6. Place the sandwiches carefully onto the bottom plate.
7. Lower the lid, and gently press.
8. Allow the sandwich to cook for 4-5 minutes.
9. Open the lid, transfer to a serving plate, cut in half, and serve. Enjoy!

Nutrition Info: Calories 625 ;Total Fats 46g ;Carbs 29g ;Protein 22g ;Fiber: 2g

Cheesy Buffalo Avocado Sandwich

Servings: 4

Cooking Time: 4 Minutes

Ingredients:

- 1 Avocado
- 2 Bread Slices
- 2 slices Cheddar Cheese
- 1 tbsp Butter
- Buffalo Sauce:
- 4 tbsp Hot Sauce
- 1 tbs White Vinegar
- ¼ cup Butter
- ¼ tsp Salt
- 1 tsp Cayenne Pepper
- ¼ tsp Garlic Salt

Directions:

1. Preheat your grill to 375 degrees F.
2. Meanwhile, peel the avocado, scoop out the flash, and mash it with a fork.
3. Spread the avocado onto a bread slice, and top with the cheddar cheese.
4. Spread the butter onto the outside of the other bread slice.
5. Top the sandwich with the buttery slice, with the butter-side up.
6. Grease the bottom cooking plate and place the sandwich there, with the butter-side up.
7. Lower the lid, press, and let the sandwich grill for about 4 minutes.
8. Meanwhile, whisk together all of the sauce ingredients.
9. Serve the sandwich with the Buffalo sauce and enjoy!

Nutrition Info: Calories 485 ;Total Fats 24g ;Carbs 35g ;Protein 8g ;Fiber: 3g

SNACK & DESSERT RECIPES

Marshmallow Stuffed Banana

Servings: 1

Cooking Time: 8 Minutes

Ingredients:

- ¼ cup of chocolate chips
- 1 banana
- ¼ cup mini marshmallows

Directions:

1. Place a peeled banana over a 12 x 12-inch foil sheet.
2. Make a slit in the banana lengthwise and stuff this slit with chocolate chips and marshmallows.
3. Wrap the foil around the banana and seal it.
4. Turn the "Selector" knob to the "Griddle" side.
5. Prepare and preheat the bottom plate of Presto Electric Griddle at 300 degrees F.
6. Once it is preheated, open the lid and place the banana in the Griddler.
7. Cook the banana in the Griddler for 4 minutes, flip and cook for another 4 minutes.
8. Unwrap and serve.

Nutrition Info: (Per Serving): Calories 372 ;Total Fat 11.8 g ;Saturated Fat 4.4 g ;Cholesterol 62 mg ;Sodium 871 mg ;Total Carbs 45.8 g ;Fiber 0.6 g ;Sugar 27.3 g ;Protein 4 g

Fruit Kabobs

Servings: 6

Cooking Time: 9 Minutes

Ingredients:

- 1 tablespoon butter
- 1/2 cup apricot preserves
- 1 tablespoon water
- 1/8 teaspoon ground cinnamon
- 1/8 teaspoon ground nutmeg
- 3 nectarines, quartered
- 3 peaches, quartered
- 3 plums, quartered
- 1 loaf (10 ¾ oz.) lb. cake, cubed

Directions:

1. Take the first five ingredients in a small saucepan and stir cook for 3 minutes on medium heat.
2. Alternately thread the lb. cake and fruits on the skewers.
3. Brush these skewers with the apricot mixture.
4. Turn the "Selector" knob to the "Grill Panini" side.
5. Preheat the bottom grill of Presto Electric Griddle at 350 degrees F and the upper grill plate on medium heat.
6. Once it is preheated, open the lid and place the fruit skewers in the Griddler.
7. Close the griddler's lid and grill the skewers for 4-6 minutes until lightly charred.
8. Serve.

Nutrition Info: (Per Serving): Calories 248 ;Total Fat 15.7 g ;Saturated Fat 2.7 g ;Cholesterol 75 mg ;Sodium 94 mg ;Total Carbs 38.4 g ;Fiber 0.3 g ;Sugar 10.1 g ;Protein 14.1 g

Banana Butter Kabobs

Servings: 6
Cooking Time: 3 Minutes
Ingredients:

- 1 loaf (10 ¾ oz.) cake, cubed
- 2 large bananas, one-inch slices
- 1/4 cup butter, melted
- 2 tablespoons brown sugar
- 1/2 teaspoon vanilla extract
- 1/8 teaspoon ground cinnamon
- 4 cups butter pecan ice cream
- 1/2 cup butterscotch ice cream topping
- 1/2 cup pecans, chopped and toasted

Directions:

1. Thread the cake and bananas over the skewers alternately.
2. Whisk butter with cinnamon, vanilla, and brown sugar in a small bowl.
3. Brush this mixture over the skewers liberally.
4. Turn the "Selector" knob to the "Grill Panini" side.
5. Preheat the bottom grill of Presto Electric Griddle at 300 degrees F and the upper grill plate on medium heat.
6. Once it is preheated, open the lid and place the banana skewers in the Griddler.
7. Close the griddler's lid and grill the skewers for 3 minutes.
8. Serve with ice cream, pecan, and butterscotch topping on top.

Nutrition Info: (Per Serving): Calories 419 ;Total Fat 19.7 g ;Saturated Fat 18.6 g ;Cholesterol 141 mg ;Sodium 193 mg ;Total Carbs 23.7 g ;Fiber 0.9 g ;Sugar 19.3 g ;Protein 5.2 g

Blueberry Cream Cheese Pancakes

Servings: 2
Cooking Time: 4 Minutes

Ingredients:

- 1 egg, beaten
- 1/3 cup Mozzarella cheese, shredded
- 1 teaspoon cream cheese, softened
- 1 teaspoon all-purpose flour
- ¼ teaspoon baking powder
- ¾ teaspoon powdered sugar
- ¼ teaspoon ground cinnamon
- ¼ teaspoon vanilla extract
- Pinch of salt
- 1 tablespoon fresh blueberries

Directions:

1. Turn the "Selector" knob to the "Griddle" side.
2. Preheat the bottom plate of the Cuisine GR Griddler at 350 degrees F.
3. In a bowl, place all ingredients except for blueberries and beat until well combined.
4. Fold in the blueberries.
5. Pour 1/2 of the mixture into preheated Griddler and cook for about 2 minutes per side.
6. Cook more pancakes using the remaining batter.
7. Serve warm.

Nutrition Info: (Per Serving): Calories 90 ;Total Fat 5 g ;Saturated Fat 2.7 g ;Cholesterol 97 mg ;Sodium 161 mg ;Total Carbs 25.7 g ;Fiber 2.8 g ;Sugar 1.2 g ;Protein 5.7 g

Grilled Peaches

Servings: 4

Cooking Time: 4 Minutes

Ingredients:

- 4 ripe peaches, halved and pitted
- 2 tablespoons maple syrup

Directions:

1. Place the water tray in the bottom of Presto Electric Griddle.
2. Place about 2 cups of lukewarm water into the water tray.
3. Place the drip pan over water tray and then arrange the heating element.
4. Now, place the grilling pan over heating element.
5. Plugin the Presto Electric Griddle and press the 'Power' button to turn it on.
6. Then press 'Fan" button.
7. Set the temperature settings according to manufacturer's directions.
8. Cover the grill with lid and let it preheat.
9. After preheating, remove the lid and grease the grilling pan.
10. Place the peach halves over the grilling pan, flesh side down.
11. Cover with the lid and cook for about 3-4 minutes.
12. Drizzle with maple syrup and serve.

Nutrition Info: (Per Serving):Calories 110 ;Total Fat 0.4 g ;Saturated Fat 0 g ;Cholesterol 0 mg ;Sodium 2 mg ;Total Carbs 27.2 g ;Fiber 2.3 g ;Sugar 25.7 g ;Protein 1.4 g

Cinnamon Pancakes

Servings: 2

Cooking Time: 4 Minutes

Ingredients:

- 1 large egg, beaten
- ¾ cup mozzarella cheese, shredded
- ½ tablespoon unsalted butter, melted
- 2 tablespoons all-purpose flour
- 2 tablespoons sugar
- ½ teaspoon ground cinnamon
- ½ teaspoon psyllium husk powder
- ¼ teaspoon baking powder
- ½ teaspoon vanilla extract
- For Topping:
- 1 teaspoon powdered sugar
- ¾ teaspoon ground cinnamon

Directions:

1. Turn the "Selector" knob to the "Griddle" side.
2. Preheat the bottom plate of the Cuisine GR Griddler at 350 degrees F.
3. In a medium bowl, put all ingredients and with a fork, mix until well combined.
4. Pour ¼ of the mixture into preheated Griddler and cook for about 2 minutes per side.
5. Cook more pancakes using the remaining batter.
6. Meanwhile, for topping: in a small bowl, mix together the sugar and cinnamon.
7. Place the pancakes onto serving plates and set aside to cool slightly.
8. Sprinkle with the cinnamon mixture and serve immediately.

Nutrition Info: (Per Serving): Calories 242 ;Total Fat 10.6 g ;Saturated Fat 4 g ;Cholesterol 106 mg ;Sodium 122 mg ;Total Carbs 24.1 g ;Fiber 2 g ;Sugar 0.3 g ;Protein 7.7 g

Blueberry Waffles

Servings: 4
Cooking Time: 6 Minutes
Ingredients:
- ¼ cup all-purpose flour
- 1 teaspoon baking powder
- 2 tablespoons butter, melted
- 2 large eggs
- 2 ounces blueberry preserves
- ¼ cup powdered sugar
- 1½ teaspoons vanilla extract

Directions:
1. Turn the "Selector" knob to the "Grill Panini" side.
2. Fix a waffle plates in the cuisine gr Griddler, preheat it at 350 degrees F and preheat the upper plate on medium heat.
3. In a bowl, add the butter and eggs and beat until creamy.
4. Add the blueberry preserves, sugar, vanilla extract and salt and beat until well combined.
5. Add the flour and baking powder and beat until well combined.
6. Pour ¼ of the mixture into preheated Griddler, close the lid and cook for about 3 minutes.
7. Cook for waffle using the remaining batter.
8. Serve warm.

Nutrition Info: (Per Serving): Calories 215 ;Total Fat 8.5 g ;Saturated Fat 9.1 g ;Cholesterol 116 mg ;Sodium 131 mg ;Total Carbs 21.6 g ;Fiber 1.1 g ;Sugar 4.7 g ;Protein 3.8 g

Walnut Pumpkin Pancakes

Servings: 2

Cooking Time: 4 Minutes

Ingredients:

- 1 egg, beaten
- ½ cup Mozzarella cheese, shredded
- 2 tablespoons all-purpose flour
- 1 tablespoon sugar-free pumpkin puree
- 1 teaspoon Sugar
- ¼ teaspoon ground cinnamon
- 2 tablespoons walnuts, toasted and chopped

Directions:

1. Turn the "Selector" knob to the "Griddle" side.
2. Preheat the bottom plate of the Cuisine GR Griddler at 350 degrees F.
3. In a bowl, add all ingredients except pecans and beat until well combined.
4. Fold in the walnuts.
5. Pour ½ of the mixture into preheated Griddler and cook for about 2 minutes per side.
6. Cook more pancakes using the remaining batter.
7. Serve warm.

Nutrition Info: (Per Serving): Calories 148 ;Total Fat 11.8 g ;Saturated Fat 2 g ;Cholesterol 86 mg ;Sodium 74 mg ;Total Carbs 23.3 g ;Fiber 1.7 g ;Sugar 0.8 g ;Protein 6.7 g

Grilled Apples

Servings: 4

Cooking Time: 7 Minutes

Ingredients:

- 2 firm tart-sweet apples, sliced
- 2 tablespoons butter, melted
- 2 tablespoons brown sugar
- 2 tablespoons white sugar
- 1 teaspoon cinnamon
- 1/4 teaspoon ginger
- 1/4 teaspoon nutmeg

Directions:

1. Mix sugar with butter, ginger, nutmeg, and cinnamon in a bowl.
2. Turn the "Selector" knob to the "Grill Panini" side.
3. Preheat the bottom grill of Presto Electric Griddle at 350 degrees F and the upper grill plate on medium heat.
4. Once it is preheated, open the lid and place the apple slices in the Griddler.
5. Close the griddler's lid and grill the apples for 7 minutes.
6. Drizzle cinnamon butter on top and serve.

Nutrition Info: (Per Serving): Calories 319 ;Total Fat 11.9 g ;Saturated Fat 1.7 g ;Cholesterol 78 mg ;Sodium 79 mg ;Total Carbs 14.8 g ;Fiber 1.1 g ;Sugar 8.3 g ;Protein 5 g

Nectarine

Servings: 2

Cooking Time: 6 Minutes

Ingredients:

- 2 medium nectarines, halved and pitted
- 1 tablespoon butter, melted
- 2 tablespoons honey
- ½ teaspoon ground nutmeg

Directions:

1. Brush the nectarine halves with butter evenly.
2. Place the water tray in the bottom of Presto Electric Griddle.
3. Place about 2 cups of lukewarm water into the water tray.
4. Place the drip pan over water tray and then arrange the heating element.
5. Now, place the grilling pan over heating element.
6. Plugin the Presto Electric Griddle and press the 'Power' button to turn it on.
7. Then press 'Fan" button.
8. Set the temperature settings according to manufacturer's directions.
9. Cover the grill with lid and let it preheat.
10. After preheating, remove the lid and grease the grilling pan.
11. Place the nectarine halves over the grilling pan.
12. Cook, uncovered for about 5-6 minutes, flipping and brushing with honey occasionally.
13. Transfer the nectarine halves onto a platter and set aside to cool.
14. Sprinkle with nutmeg and serve.

Nutrition Info: (Per Serving):Calories 180 ;Total Fat 6.4 g ;Saturated Fat 3.8 g ;Cholesterol 15 mg ;Sodium 42 mg ;Total Carbs 32.6 g ;Fiber 2.6 g ;Sugar 28.6 g ;Protein 1.7 g

Veggie Sliders

Servings: 10

Cooking Time: 7 Minutes

Ingredients:

- ½ Red Onion, diced
- ¾ cup cooked Quinoa
- 15 ounces canned Kidney
- ½ cup Walnuts, crushed or ground
- 1 shake Worcestershire Sauce
- 1 tbsp Chili Powder
- Salt and Pepper, to taste

Directions:

1. Preheat your grill to 350-375 degrees F.
2. Dump all of the ingredients in a bowl and mix well with your hands to incorporate the mixture.
3. Make about 10 small patties with your hands.
4. When ready, open the grill and coat with cooking spray.
5. Arrange the patties on top of the bottom plate.
6. Lower the lid and cook closed for about 6-7 minutes.
7. Serve on top of a lettuce leaf. Enjoy!

Nutrition Info: Calories 89 ;Total Fats 4.2g ;Carbs 9g ;Protein 4g ;Fiber: 3g

Made in United States
Troutdale, OR
04/21/2024

19323024R10060